TEACHER'S PET PUBLICATIONS

LITPLAN TEACHER PACK
for
Farewell to Manzanar
based on the book by
Jeanne Wakatsuki Houston & James D. Houston

Written by
Barbara M. Linde, MA Ed.

© 2004 Teacher's Pet Publications
All Rights Reserved

This Lit Plan on *Farewell to Manzanar* has been brought to you
by Teacher's Pet Publications, Inc.

Copyright Teacher's Pet Publications 2004
All Rights Reserved

Only the student materials in this unit plan may be reproduced.
Pages such as worksheets and study guides may be reproduced
for use in the purchaser's classroom.
For any additional copyright questions, contact Teacher's Pet Publications.

www.tpet.com

TABLE OF CONTENTS – *Farewell to Manzanar*

Introduction	7
Unit Objectives	10
Reading Assignment Sheet	11
Unit Outline	12
Study Questions	15
Quiz/Study Questions (Multiple Choice)	28
Pre-Reading Vocabulary Worksheets	49
Lesson One (Introductory Lesson)	69
Nonfiction Assignment Sheet	74
Oral Reading Evaluation Form	75
Writing Assignment 1	79
Writing Evaluation Form	80
Writing Assignment 2	85
Extra Writing Assignments/Discussion Questions	90
Writing Assignment 3	93
Vocabulary Review Activities	95
Unit Review Activities	96
Unit Tests	103
Unit Resource Materials	143
Vocabulary Resource Materials	173

A FEW NOTES ABOUT THE AUTHOR
JEANNE WAKATSUKI HOUSTON

HOUSTON, Jeanne (Toyo) Wakatsuki (1934--) Jeanne (Toyo) Wakatsuki was born on September 26, 1934 in Inglewood, California. Her father, Ko, was born in Hiroshima, Japan and was a first-generation Japanese immigrant to America. Her mother, Riku was born in Hawaii and was a second generation Japanese-American. Jeanne was the youngest of the children. She had five older sisters and four older brothers.

The Wakatsuki family was part of the 110,000 Japanese Americans who were interned in relocation camps during World War II. *Farewell to Manzanar*, written in 1973 by Jeanne and her husband, James Houston, is the story of her family's time at the camp. After being released from the camp in 1945, Jeanne moved back to the Los Angeles area with her parents and some of her siblings. She studied sociology and journalism at San Jose State College in San Jose, California. She met James Houston while in college and married him in 1957.

In 1971 one of her nephews asked Jeanne for details about Manzanar, as he had been born there but did not have many memories of the experience. In 1972, thirty years after leaving Manzanar, Jeanne returned to the Manzanar campsite with her husband and three daughters. This visit helped her come to terms with what had happened to her and her family. Jeanne and her husband began writing *Farewell to Manzanar* together. She documents the return visit in the last chapter of the book.

Jeanne Wakatsuki Houston continues to write and lecture on her works and her life experiences. She lives in Santa Cruz, California, with her family. Her other books are *The Legend of Fire Horse Woman, Beyond Manzanar*, and *Don't Cry, It's Only Thunder*. Along with her husband, she wrote the screenplay for the film version of Farewell to Manzanar. This was a made-for-TV movie that was shown in 1976. The couple's twin daughters appeared in the movie. The screenplay won the Christopher Award and the Humanities Prize. In 1984 she received the National Women's Political Caucus award and the Wonder woman award.

HOUSTON, James D. (1933 --) James Houston was born in San Francisco, California, in 1933. He met Jeanne Wakatsuki while attending San Jose State College, and married her in 1957. He has taught at the University of California at Santa Cruz and at Stanford University. Houston's other books include **A Native Son of the Golden West**, *Continental Drift,* and *In the Ring of Fire*. He has been awarded the Wallace Stenger Writing Fellowship at Stanford University and has won the Joseph Henry Jackson Award for Fiction and other awards.

INTRODUCTION - *Farewell to Manzanar*

This unit has been designed to develop students' reading, writing, thinking, listening, and speaking skills through exercises and activities related to *Farewell to Manzanar* by Jeanne Wakatsuki Houston It includes 20 lessons, supported by extra resource materials.

The **introductory lesson** introduces students to *Farewell to Manzanar*. Following the introductory activity, students are given an explanation of how the activity relates to the book they are about to read. Following the transition, students are given the materials they will be using during the unit. They are also introduced to the nonfiction assignment. At the end of the lesson, students begin the pre-reading work for the first reading assignment.

The **reading assignments** are approximately 30 pages each; some are a little shorter while others are a little longer. Students have approximately 15 minutes of pre-reading work to do prior to each reading assignment. This pre-reading work involves reviewing the study questions for the assignment and doing some vocabulary work for 8 to 10 vocabulary words they will encounter in their reading.

The **study guide questions** are fact-based questions; students can find the answers to these questions right in the text. These questions come in two formats: short answer or multiple choice. The best use of these materials is probably to use the short answer version of the questions as study guides for students (since answers will be more complete), and to use the multiple-choice version for occasional quizzes. It might be a good idea to make transparencies of your answer keys for the overhead projector.

The **vocabulary work** is intended to enrich students' vocabularies as well as to aid in the students' understanding of the book. Prior to each reading assignment, students will complete a two-part worksheet for approximately 8 to 10 vocabulary words in the upcoming reading assignment. Part I focuses on students' use of general knowledge and contextual clues by giving the sentence in which the word appears in the text. Students are then to write down what they think the words mean based on the words' usage. Part II gives students dictionary definitions of the words and has them match the words to the correct definitions based on the words' contextual usage. Students should then have an understanding of the words when they meet them in the text.

After each reading assignment, students will go back and formulate answers for the study guide questions. Discussion of these questions serves as a **review** of the most important events and ideas presented in the reading assignments.

After students complete extra discussion questions, there is a **vocabulary review** lesson which pulls together all of the separate vocabulary lists for the reading assignments and gives students a review of all of the words they have studied.

Following the reading of the book, two lessons are devoted to the **extra discussion questions/writing assignments**. These questions focus on interpretation, critical analysis and personal response, employing a variety of thinking skills and adding to the students' understanding of the novel. These questions are done as a **group activity**.

Using the information they have acquired so far through individual work and class discussions, students get together to further examine the text and to brainstorm ideas relating to the themes of the novel.

The group activity is followed by a **reports and discussion** session in which the groups share their ideas about the book with the entire class; thus, the entire class gets exposed to many different ideas regarding the themes and events of the book.

There are three **writing assignments** in this unit, each with the purpose of informing, persuading, or having students express personal opinions. The first assignment is to **inform.** Students will write a newspaper article related to the internment of the Japanese-Americans. The second writing assignment is to **persuade**. Students will write a letter to a government official explaining why the Japanese-Americans should be released from the internment camps. The third writing assignment is to offer a **personal opinion.** Students will take the role of a friend of Jeanne's in junior high or high school and tell other students how Jeanne should be treated. .

In addition, there is a **nonfiction reading assignment**. Students are required to read a piece of nonfiction related in some way to *Farewell to Manzanar*. After reading their nonfiction pieces, students will fill out a worksheet on which they answer questions regarding facts, interpretation, criticism, and personal opinions. During one class period, students make **oral presentations** about the nonfiction pieces they have read. This not only exposes all students to a wealth of information; it also gives students the opportunity to practice **public speaking**.

The **review lesson** pulls together all of the aspects of the unit. The teacher is given four or five choices of activities or games to use which all serve the same basic function of reviewing all of the information presented in the unit.

The **unit test** comes in two formats: all multiple choice matching true/false or with a mixture of matching, short answer, and composition. As a convenience, two different tests for each format have been included.

There are additional **support materials** included with this unit. The **resource materials sections** include suggestions for an in-class library, crossword and word search puzzles related to the novel, and extra vocabulary worksheets. There is a list of **bulletin board ideas** which gives the teacher suggestions for bulletin boards to go along with this unit. In addition, there is a list of **extra class activities** the teacher could choose from to enhance the unit or as a substitution for an exercise the teacher might feel is inappropriate for his/her class. **Answer keys** are located directly after the **reproducible student materials** throughout the unit.

UNIT PLAN ADAPTATIONS - *Farewell to Manzanar*

<u>Block Schedule</u>

Depending on the length of your class periods, and the frequency with which the class meets, you may wish to choose one of the following options:
- Complete two of the daily lessons in one class period.
- Have students complete all reading and writing activities in class.
- Assign all reading to be completed out of class, and concentrate on the worksheets and discussions in class.
- Assign the projects from Daily Lesson Fifteen at the beginning of the unit, and allow time each day for students to work on them.
- Use some of the Unit and Vocabulary Resource activities during every class.

<u>Gifted & Talented / Advanced Classes</u>
- Emphasize the projects and the extra discussion questions.
- Have students complete all of the writing activities.
- Assign the reading to be completed out of class and focus on the discussions in class.
- Encourage students to develop their own questions.

<u>ESL / ELD</u>
- Assign a partner to help the student read the text aloud.
- Tape record the text and have the student listen and follow along in the text.
- Give the student the study guide worksheets to use as they read.
- Provide pictures and demonstrations to explain difficult vocabulary words and concepts.
- Conduct guided reading lessons, asking students to stop frequently and explain what they have read.

UNIT OBJECTIVES - *Farewell to Manzanar*

1. Through reading *Farewell to Manzanar* students will analyze characters and their situations to better understand the themes of the novel.

2. Students will demonstrate their understanding of the text on four levels: factual, interpretive, critical, and personal.

3. Students will practice reading aloud and silently to improve their skills in each area.

4. Students will enrich their vocabularies and improve their understanding of the novel through the vocabulary lessons prepared for use in conjunction with it.

5. Students will answer questions to demonstrate their knowledge and understanding of the main events and characters in *Farewell to Manzanar.*

6. Students will practice writing through a variety of writing assignments.

7. The writing assignments in this are geared to several purposes:
    a. To check the students' reading comprehension
    b. To make students think about the ideas presented by the novel
    c. To make students put those ideas into perspective
    d. To encourage critical and logical thinking
    e. To provide the opportunity to practice good grammar and improve students' use of the English language.

8. Students will read aloud, report, and participate in large and small group discussions to improve their public speaking and personal interaction skills.

READING ASSIGNMENT SHEET
Farewell to Manzanar

Date Assigned	Reading Assignment	Completion Date
	Forward, Chronology, Terms	
	Part I: Chapters 1, 2, 3	
	Part I: Chapters 4, 5. 6	
	Part I: Chapters 7, 8, 9, 10, 11	
	Part I: Chapters 12, 13, 14, 15	
	Part I: Chapters 16, 17, 18, 19	
	Part II: Chapters 20, 21	
	Part III: Chapter 22	

WRITING ASSIGNMENT LOG
Farewell to Manzanar

Date Assigned	Assignment	Completion Date
	Writing Assignment 1	
	Writing Assignment 2	
	Writing Assignment 3	
	Non-fiction Assignment	

UNIT OUTLINE - *Farewell to Manzanar*

1 Introduction PV Foreword, Chronology, Terms	2 R Study?? F, C, T Nonfiction Assignment	3 PVR Study?? I: 1, 2, 3 Oral Reading Evaluation	4 PVR Study?? I: 4, 5, 6	5 Writing Assignment #1
6 PVR Study?? I: 7-11	7 Quiz I: 1-11 Writing Assignment # 2	8 PVR II: 12-15	9 Writing Conference Study?? II: 12-15	10 PVR Study?? II: 16-19
11 PVR II: 20-21	12 Study?? II: 20-21 PVR III: 22	13 Study ?? III: 22 Extra Discussion ??	14 Writing Assignment #3	15 Library Work
16 Vocabulary Review	17 Unit Review	18 Test	19 Nonfiction Assignment	20 Film, Audiocassette

Key: P = Preview Study Questions V = Vocabulary Work R = Read

STUDY GUIDE QUESTIONS

SHORT ANSWER STUDY GUIDE QUESTIONS - *Farewell to Manzanar*

Foreword, Chronology, and Terms
1. What is the author's (Jeanne Wakatsuki Houston) relationship to Manzanar?
2. When did the first Japanese arrive on the US mainland, and where did they settle?
3. When did Congress grant naturalization rights to some groups? Which groups were granted the rights? Which groups were omitted?
4. When did the Japanese government lift its ban on emigration, and what was the result?
5. What restriction did the U. S. Bureau of Immigration and Naturalization create for the Japanese, and when was this done?
6. When and why did immigration from Japan to the United States stop?
7. When was the attack on Pearl Harbor?
8. Describe the three events that occurred in 1942.
9. Describe the Supreme Court ruling of 1944 and the two events of 1945. Include the dates.
10. What is Public Law 414, and when was it passed?

Part I: Chapters 1, 2, 3
1. What is the setting when the story opens?
2. Why did the fishing boats return?
3. What did Papa do the night he heard the news?
4. Why was the FBI picking up Japanese-American fishermen?
5. What happened to Papa two weeks later, and how did he react?
6. Why was Jeanne afraid on Terminal Island?
7. What was Order 9066 and how did it affect the Japanese Americans?
8. How does Jeanne describe the public attitudes toward the Japanese in California? Include the example of her teacher in Boyle Heights.
9. What happened to the Wakatsuki family?
10. Describe the conditions in the barracks.

Part I: Chapters 4, 5, 6
1. How was the War Department helping the people in the camps to get better clothing?
2. What was Jeanne's physical condition at the camp?
3. What is Jeanne's observation of how Mama coped with using the latrines?
4. How does Jeanne describe the entire situation?
5. What happened in the mess halls that changed the families? Why did this happen?
6. What work did Mama start doing? Why was she doing it?
7. How old is the author in this part of the story?
8. Describe the reunion with Papa. Include how he looked and what Jeanne did.
9. How does Jeanne as an adult see the cane that Papa brought back with him from Fort Lincoln?
10. What job did Papa have at Fort Lincoln? Why did he have that job?

Short Answer Study Guide Questions *Farewell to Manzanar*

Part I: Chapters 7, 8, 9, 10, 11
1. The interrogator asked Papa what he thought of the Japanese attack on Pearl Harbor. What was Papa's response?
2. Why were the women calling papa "inu"?
3. Summarize the scene in Chapter 8 where Papa attacked Mama. Explain why this attack was different from previous ones.
4. Why wouldn't Papa or most of the other Japanese-American men talk about Fort Lincoln?
5. Who was Fred Tayama? Why and when he was beaten?
6. Describe the riot. Include the causes, results, and the name of the leader.
7. Describe the events that took place in the reservoir shack.
8. What two questions were on the Loyalty Oath?
9. How does Jeanne describe the results of the Loyalty Oath?
10. How did Papa answer the questions on the Loyalty Oath? Why did he answer that way?

Part II: Chapters 12, 13, 14, 15
1. The word *manzanar* is Spanish. What is the English translation of the word? Why was Manzanar so named?
2. What did the trees symbolize for Jeanne?
3. How did life in the camp change after the fist year?
4. What activities was papa doing?
5. What did the residents do to make the camp livable?
6. What does Jeanne say the camp became as the months turned into years? Explain what she meant by this.
7. What would Jeanne have done if she had been told she was free? Why did she say she would act so?
8. How did Jeanne describe ballet before and after the demonstration by the dancer? Include
9. What was Papa's reaction when Jeanne said she wanted to be baptized and confirmed Catholic? Why did he react that way? Did Jeanne follow through with her plan?
10. What happened to Woody? How did Jeanne feel about it?

Part II: Chapters 16, 17, 18, 19
1. Describe the first two Supreme Court cases involving the camps.
2. Describe the Supreme Court case called *Ex Parte Endo* and the ruling that resulted from it. Include the meaning of the term *habeas corpus* and the result of the ruling.
3. What problem did the family face as a result of the court ruling?

MORE ON THE NEXT PAGE

Short Answer Study Guide Questions *Farewell to Manzanar*

Part II: Chapters 16, 17, 18, 19, continued
4. Jeanne said she had a foretaste of being hated. How did she say she would have to respond? How did she feel about it?
5. What comparison did Jeanne use to describe Papa now?
6. Why did Papa wait for the government to arrange his departure from the camp?
7. What event finally caused the camps to be completely closed? When did this happen?
8. Describe Woody's journey in April 1946. Tell where he went, what he did, and whom he saw, and how he was treated.
9. Jeanne says the family left the camp "in style." Describe this.
10. What job did Mama take? What did Papa do after they settled into Cabrillo Homes?

Part II: Chapters 20, 21
1. What did Jeanne do on her first day in class that amazed one of the other students? What was Jeanne's reaction to the girl's comment?
2. What was Jeanne's double impulse?
3. In which areas was Jeanne allowed to perform? In which areas was there another set of rules?
4. How did Jeanne view her situation when it was happening and also as an adult looking back when she wrote the book?
5. What was the sign to Jeanne of how to cross what she called "intangible barriers?"
6. How were Papa's failures contrasted by Woody's return?
7. What happened to the relationship between Jeanne and Radine when they went to high school? Why did this happen? How did Jeanne feel about it?
8. Describe Jeanne's dream and what it meant to her.
9. What important event happened to Jeanne during her senior year in high school? What was Papa's response to the knowledge of this event? How did Jeanne respond?
10. Describe coronation night. Include a description of Jeanne's dress.

Part III: Chapter 22
1. How long did it take Jeanne to get the confidence to deal with Manzanar?
2. What family "firsts" did Jeanne accomplish?
3. Where did Jeanne go in April 1972? Who went with her?
4. What did the place look like?
5. What did Jeanne feel and hear?
6. What was Jeanne thinking about as she looked around?
7. What inscription did Jeanne read on the flagpole circle and what was the significance?
8. What was Jeanne thinking about her oldest daughter?
9. How did the trip help Jeanne?
10 What did Jeanne remember, and what did it signify?

ANSWER KEY: SHORT ANSWER STUDY GUIDE QUESTIONS - *Farewell to Manzanar*

Foreword, Chronology, and Terms

1. What is the author's (Jeanne Wakatsuki Houston) relationship to Manzanar?
    She was interred there with her family when she was a young girl.

2. When did the first Japanese arrive on the US mainland, and where did they settle?
    They arrived at Gold Hill near Sacramento, CA in 1869.

3. When did Congress grant naturalization rights to some groups? Which groups were granted the rights? Which groups were omitted?
    In 1870, Congress granted naturalization rights to free whites and people of African descent, but not to the Oriental races.

4. When did the Japanese government lift its ban on emigration, and what was the result?
    In 1886 the Japanese government lifted its ban on emigration. As a result, Japanese citizens were able for the first time to move to other countries.

5. What restriction did the U. S. Bureau of Immigration and Naturalization create for the Japanese, and when was this done?
    In 1911 the U. S. Bureau of Immigration and Naturalization said that only whites and people of African descent could file for citizenship. The Japanese were not allowed to file for U. S. citizenship.

6. When and why did immigration from Japan to the United States stop?
    In 1924 The U. S. Congress passed an Immigration Act that said any immigrant who could not become an U. S. citizen could not enter the United States. This meant that no Japanese could enter the country.

7. When was the attack on Pearl Harbor?
    December 7, 1941

8. Describe the three events that occurred in 1942.
    1. February 19. President Roosevelt gives the War Department the authority to define military areas in the western states and to exclude anyone who might be a threat.
    2. March 25. Evacuees begin to arrive at the Manzanar camp.
    3. August 12. Evacuation of 110,000 people of Japanese ancestry to ten inland camps is completed.

9. Describe the Supreme Court ruling of 1944 and the two events of 1945. Include the dates.
    December 18, 1944. The U.S. Supreme Court rules that loyal citizens cannot be held in detention camps.
    August 14, 1945. Japan surrenders and World War II ends.
    November 21, 1945. The Manzanar camp officially closes.

10. What is Public Law 414, and when was it passed?
    Public Law 414 was passed in 1952. It granted Japanese aliens the right to become naturalized United States citizens.

Part I: Chapters 1, 2, 3
1. What is the setting when the story opens?
    The wharf in Long Beach, California, in 1941.

2. Why did the fishing boats return?
    They had heard on their radios that the Japanese had bombed Pearl Harbor.

3. What did Papa do the night he heard the news?
    He burned the flag from Hiroshima, papers, documents, and anything that would show a connection with Japan.

4. Why was the FBI picking up Japanese-American fishermen?
    The FBI thought the Japanese-American fishermen might be contacting enemy Japanese ships off the western coast of the US.

5. What happened to Papa two weeks later, and how did he react?
    He was arrested by the FBI. He maintained his dignity and led the agents out of his house.

6. Why was Jeanne afraid on Terminal Island?
    It was the first time she had lived or gone to school with other Japanese people. When she was young, her father used to tell her he would sell her to the Chinamen if she misbehaved. So she was afraid of the other Japanese people.

7. What was Order 9066 and how did it affect the Japanese Americans?
    Order 9066 authorized the War Department to define military areas in the western states and to exclude anyone who might be considered a threat to the war effort. The Japanese were talking about the possibility that they would be moved to some place inland.

8. How does Jeanne describe the public attitudes toward the Japanese in California? Include the example of her teacher in Boyle Heights.
   The teacher ignored Jeanne. This was the first time she felt open hostility from a Caucasian.

9. What happened to the Wakatsuki family?
   They were relocated to the Manzanar camp.

10. Describe the conditions in the barracks.
    The barracks had been divided into small units and were crowded. Dust and wind blew in from the outside through cracks in the walls. The only furniture was Army surplus cots, blankets, and mattress covers.

Part I: Chapters 4, 5, 6
1. How was the War Department helping the people in the camps to get better clothing?
   The War Department issued military surplus clothing to the people in the camp. They also brought in sewing machines and turned one barracks into a clothing factory.

2. What was Jeanne's physical condition at the camp?
   She was sick continually, with stomach cramps and diarrhea.

3. What is Jeanne's observation of how Mama coped with using the latrines?
   It was a humiliation that Mama endured but never got used to. She cooperated to survive but still tried to keep her personal privacy.

4. How does Jeanne describe the entire situation?
   "All this was an open insult to the private self, a slap in the face you were powerless to challenge."

5. What happened in the mess halls that changed the families? Why did this happen?
   In the mess halls they stopped eating as a family. Granny was not able to walk to the mess hall, so Mama brought her food to the barracks. The children ate with their friends. Sometimes the children went to a different block if they heard the cook there was good. After three years of eating in the mess hall, Jeanne's family collapsed as an integrated unit.

6. What work did Mama start doing? Why was she doing it?
   Mama went to work as a dietician. She made money to pay the monthly fee for the warehouse where she had stored her things.

7. How old is the author in this part of the story?
>She is seven years old.

8. Describe the reunion with Papa. Include how he looked and what Jeanne did.
>After nine months, Papa came to the camp by Greyhound bus. Everyone lined up to meet him. He looked like he was ten years older. He was thin and leaned on his cane. No one said anything. Then Jeanne hugged him and cried. Then everyone cried.

9. How does Jeanne as an adult see the cane that Papa brought back with him from Fort Lincoln?
>She sees the cane as "a sad, homemade version of the samurai sword his grandfather carried in the land around Hiroshima."

10. What job did Papa have at Fort Lincoln? Why did he have that job?
>He was an interviewer for the Justice Department because he spoke Japanese and English.

Part I: Chapters 7, 8, 9, 10, 11

1. The interrogator asked Papa what he thought of the Japanese attack on Pearl Harbor. What was Papa's response?
>Papa said he was sad for both countries; that the bombing and war were the things that happened when military men were in control.

2. Why were the women calling papa "inu"?
>The word *inu* means collaborator or informer. Anyone who cooperated with the camp authorities was considered *inu*. Papa had been released from Fort Lincoln earlier than some of the other men because the Justice Department could not find any reason to keep him. When he got to Manzanar, a rumor went around the camp that when he was interpreting for the military authorities at Fort Lincoln he got information from other Japanese prisoners and gave it to the authorities to buy his release. None of this was true.

3. Summarize the scene in Chapter 8 where Papa attacked Mama. Explain why this attack was different from previous ones.
>Papa was drunk when Jeanne and Mama returned to the barracks one evening. He yelled at Mama for disturbing him, not bringing his food on time, and bringing too much cabbage and not enough rice. He threatened to kill her with his cane and she told him to go ahead. At that point Kiyo intervened and stopped Papa by punching him in the face. To Jeanne it seemed like the center of her world had collapsed when Papa lost his authority in the family.

4. Why wouldn't Papa or most of the other Japanese men talk about Fort Lincoln?
   The men were charged with disloyalty to the American government. For a Japanese man, disloyalty was the greatest possible disgrace. They were also humiliated at their powerlessness.

5. Who was Fred Tayama? Why and when he was beaten? What happened to the men who beat him?

   Fred was the leader of the Japanese American Citizens League at the camp. He was friendly with the camp administrators. On the night of December 5, Fred was beaten by six men but could not identify them.

6. Describe the riot. Include the causes, results, and the name of the leader.
   The day after Fred was beaten, three men were identified, and one was sent to the county jail. This man had been trying to organize a Kitchen Workers' Union in the camp. The beating and arrest caused a riot. The leader of the riot was Joe Kurihara. He demanded that the cook be brought back to the camp, and the authorities agreed. Later that same day, part of the mob went to the hospital to kill Fred Tayama. Some of the men went after others they thought were sympathizers. The part of the mob that went to the police station after the cook met up with the military police while they were still inside the camp. A fight started, and the MPs fired weapons and threw tear gas bombs. This action stopped the riot but two men died and ten were injured.

7. Describe the events that took place in the reservoir shack.
   Jeanne's brother-in-law, Kaz, was the foreman of the reservoir maintenance detail. The men on this crew were the only ones allowed outside the camp the night the riot occurred. While the men were in the shack some MPs burst in. They held the crew under armed guard until they verified that the men were allowed out of the camp.

8. What two questions were on the Loyalty Oath?
   The one question asked if the signer was willing to serve in the United States Armed Forces on combat duty. The second question asked if the signer would swear unqualified allegiance to the United States of America, defend the country from attack, and forswore any allegiance to Japan.

9. How does Jeanne describe the results of the Loyalty Oath?
   She said the results would have been comical if they had not been so grotesque. An espionage agent would not admit to being disloyal, while the Japanese who were loyal to America were so outraged at being made to take the oath that they turned anti-American.

10. How did Papa answer the questions on the Loyalty Oath? Why did he answer that way?
    Papa answered YES YES to the questions. He did this because he thought he was too old to start over if he were sent back to Japan, and to keep the family together at Manzanar. If he had answered NO NO, he would have been sent to a camp for the disloyal and eventually might have been sent back to Japan

Part II: Chapters 12, 13, 14, 15

1. The word *manzanar* is Spanish. What is the English translation of the word? Why was Manzanar so named?

    Manzanar means *"apple orchard."* The area where the Manzanar camp was located in the Owens Valley, had once been apple orchards. Around the 1920s the area turned to desert when the water flow was diverted to Los Angeles.

2. What did the trees symbolize for Jeanne?

    The family's barracks was near an old pear orchard that still had some live fruit trees. The trees symbolized the "turning of our life in the camp, from the outrageous to the tolerable." Papa pruned the trees and they picked the fruit.

3. How did life in the camp change after the fist year?

    The residents were allowed outside the wire for recreation.

4. What activities was papa doing?

    Papa collected driftwood and carved furniture and other items from it. He made a rock garden from stones he gathered in the desert. He began painting watercolors, especially of the mountains.

5. What did the residents do to make the camp livable?

    They made the best of a bad situation. They planted gardens of all kinds, started a farm outside the gate, and built a park. They had beauty parlors, scout troops, churches, police and fire departments, and many other things that would be in an American small town.

6. What does Jeanne say the camp became as the months turned into years? Explain what she meant by this.

    The camp became its own world. People seemed to forget the war and only think of the next task that had to be done. They tried to create normalcy and keep any anger under control.

7. What would Jeanne have done if she had been told she was free? Why did she say she would act so?

    She said she would go right back to the camp. The Sierra Mountains looked like a huge barricade and scared her. Death Valley was in the other direction from the camp. Also, she thought of Block 28 as her home.

8. How did Jeanne describe ballet before and after the demonstration by the dancer? Include the translation of the Japanese words *daikon ashi* that Jeanne used to describe the woman's legs.

    Before the demonstration Jeanne was interested in the toe shoes. After she watched the dancer, she thought her legs looked like horseradishes. She thought the woman was sad to watch. After the dancer took off her shoes Jeanne noticed her bloody toes. She felt sorry for the dancer, so she signed up for lessons. However, she did not return to take the lessons. She thought ballet was a misuse of the body.

9. What was Papa's reaction when Jeanne said she wanted to be baptized and confirmed Catholic? Why did he react that way? Did Jeanne follow through with her plan?

> Papa refused to give his permission and argued with the nun. He wanted Jeanne to marry a Japanese boy and said she would not be able to do that if she were Catholic, as there weren't any Japanese Catholics. Jeanne did not get baptized or confirmed.

10. What happened to Woody? How did Jeanne feel about it?

> He was drafted into the Army and left the camp with his unit. Jeanne did not understand what was happening, but she related it to the time her father left. She thought the world would end if anything happened to Woody.

Part II: Chapters 16, 17, 18, 19

1. Describe the first two Supreme Court cases involving the camps.

> The first case a Nisei student named Gordon Hirabayashi challenged the racial bias of the evacuation order, and the violation of his civil rights. He also stayed out after curfew. The court did not rule on the evacuation order but said that during wartime the army had the right to impose a curfew and place restrictions on a racial group.
> In the second case, a Nisei named Fred Korematsu challenged the racial bias of the evacuation. To avoid internment, he had had plastic surgery and changed his name. The court sided with the army and allowed the evacuations.

2. Describe the Supreme Court case called *Ex Parte Endo* and the ruling that resulted from it. Include the meaning of the term *habeas corpus* and the result of the ruling.

> The third case challenged the actual internment. In April 1942 a Nisei woman named Mitsue Endo protested the internment under the right of habeas corpus. That meant a person could not be unjustly held against their will. The court agreed that the government did not have the authority to imprison loyal citizens against their will. Because of the ruling, the army started closing the camps and told the internees they were allowed to return to their homes.

3. What problem did the family face as a result of the court ruling?

> They had nowhere to go. They were afraid to go back to the west coast because of the presence of hate groups. Violence against the Japanese Americans was going on all over the west coast.

4. Jeanne said she had a foretaste of being hated. How did she say she would have to respond? How did she feel about it?

> She said she would allow someone to look at her with hatred because she thought she must have deserved it. She felt humiliated that someone could hate her and her family. She wanted to stay inside the camp and not face the prejudice.

5. What comparison did Jeanne use to describe Papa now?
    He was like a slave who had been freed after the Civil War. He didn't know what to do next.

6. Why did Papa wait for the government to arrange his departure from the camp?
    He had nowhere to go and no job. In 1943 a California law restricted Japanese Americans from getting a commercial fishing license. He felt safer in the camp. He thought the government should take care of his departure since it had brought him there in the first place.

7. What event finally caused the camps to be completely closed? When did this happen?
    On August 6 the United States dropped the atom bomb on Hiroshima, ending the war.

8. Describe Woody's journey in April 1946. Tell where he went, what he did, and whom he saw, and how he was treated.
    Woody went to Ka-ke, Japan, the former home of their father. He visited his father's relatives. His great-aunt Toto showed Woody the place where the family had buried his father. They thought he was dead because he had not contacted them for nine years before the burial. The family members gladly welcomed him as his father's son.

9. Jeanne says the family left the camp "in style." Describe this.
    Papa bought a Nash sedan so the family could drive away from the camp.

10. What job did Mama take? What did Papa do after they settled into Cabrillo Homes?
    Mama took a job at a fish cannery. Papa drafted plans for a housing cooperative.

Part II: Chapters 20, 21
1. What did Jeanne do on her first day in class that amazed one of the other students? What was Jeanne's reaction to the girl's comment?
    Jeanne read out loud with no mistakes. One of her classmates was amazed that Jeanne spoke English. Jeanne was stunned that the girl thought she would not speak English.

2. What was Jeanne's double impulse?
    She wanted to disappear and be accepted at the same time.

3. In which areas was Jeanne allowed to perform? In which areas was there another set of rules?
    She was allowed to perform in scholarship, athletics, and school-related activities like the yearbook, newspaper, and student government. She was often not allowed to go to the homes of other students or join certain groups, like the Girl Scouts.

4. How did Jeanne view her situation when it was happening and also as an adult looking back when she wrote the book?
    When she was a child she accepted the limitations placed on her and saw the situation as her fault. She thought she was creating a problem for the others. As an adult looking back, she is infuriated that she accepted things so readily.

5. What was the sign to Jeanne of how to cross what she called "intangible barriers?"
>The Boy Scouts needed baton twirlers. Since Jeanne and her friend Radine were physically mature, and the group was run by the fathers, Jeanne and Radine were welcomed as baton twirlers. Jeanne was unconsciously learning to use her sexuality and femininity to get accepted.

6. How were Papa's failures contrasted by Woody's return?
>Papa's plans all failed. When Woody came back from Japan he had more self-confidence. Papa began to depend on Woody instead of being in charge himself.

7. What happened to the relationship between Jeanne and Radine when they went to high school? Why did this happen? How did Jeanne feel about it?
>Radine was accepted into the high school social circles but Jeanne was not. Radine also became a singer, but that role was not open to Jeanne. She felt demoralized by watching Radine's successes.

8. Describe Jeanne's dream and what it meant to her.
>In the dream Jeanne watches through a window a blond, blue-eyed high school girl is admired by others. She wants to cry because the girl is something she (Jeanne) can never be.

9. What important event happened to Jeanne during her senior year in high school? What was Papa's response to the knowledge of this event? How did Jeanne respond?
>She was elected the school carnival queen. Papa enrolled Jeanne in a traditional Japanese odori class to learn Japanese ways. Jeanne lasted for ten lessons before the teacher sent her away.

10. Describe coronation night. Include a description of Jeanne's dress.
>Jeanne's dress looked old-fashioned, with a high neck and ruffles. This contrasted sharply with her four attendants' strapless, form-fitting dresses. While she was walking to her throne she felt uncomfortable and wished she was wearing her sarong. She knew she would not be invited to the party after the coronation. She wanted to laugh and cry and be able to believe in princesses and queens.

Part III: Chapter 22

1. How long did it take Jeanne to get the confidence to deal with Manzanar?
>Twenty years.

2. What family "firsts" did Jeanne accomplish?
>She was the first to finish college, and the first to marry out of her race.

3. Where did Jeanne go in April 1972? Who went with her?
>She and her husband and children went to the site of the Manzanar camp.

4. What did the place look like?
>The buildings were all gone. Only the two gatehouses remained.

5. What did Jeanne feel and hear?
>   She heard whispers and felt the presence of those who had been at the camp and those who had died there.

6. What was Jeanne thinking about as she looked around?
>   She tried to detach from the memories and look at the area as an historical and archaeological site.

7. What inscription did Jeanne read on the flagpole circle and what was the significance?
>   The inscription said, 'BUILT BY WADA AND CREW, JUNE 10, 1942 A. D." This told Jeanne that the man who made the inscription did not want his work at the flagpole circle to be forgotten.

8. What was Jeanne thinking about her oldest daughter?
>   She realized that her daughter, at age eleven, was the same age as she was when the camp closed.

9. How did the trip help Jeanne?
>   It helped her realize that her life really began at Manzanar. The trip helped her understand the bits of the place that she still carried within her.

10 What did Jeanne remember, and what did it signify?
>   She remembered the day the family left the camp in the car her father had bought. She realized that she had always remembered her father's last act of defiance.

MULTIPLE CHOICE STUDY GUIDE/QUIZ QUESTIONS *Farewell to Manzanar*

<u>Foreword, Chronology, and Terms</u>

1. What is the author's (Jeanne Wakatsuki Houston) relationship to Manzanar?
    A. She was a reporter doing a story about the camp.
    B. Her parents were interred there before she was born.
    C. Her husband's family was interred there when he was a boy.
    D. She was interred there with her family when she was a young girl.

2. When and where did the first Japanese settle on the US mainland?
    A. They settled at Portland, Oregon, in 1818.
    B. They settled at Sacramento, CA in 1869.
    C. They settled at Seattle, Washington, in 1852.
    D. They settled at Long Beach, California in 1890.

3. In 1870 Congress granted naturalization rights to ____.
    A. Orientals only
    B. free whites, Orientals, and Mexicans
    C. free whites and people of African descent
    D. people of African descent and people from the Middle East

4. When did the Japanese government lift its ban on emigration?
    A. 1886
    B. 1914
    C. 1940
    D. 1812

5. True or False: In 1911 the U. S. Bureau of Immigration and Naturalization allowed the Japanese to file for U. S. citizenship.
    A. True
    B. False

6. When did immigration from Japan to the United States stop?
    A. 1899
    B. 1924
    C. 1942
    D. 1876

7. When was the attack on Pearl Harbor?
    A. January 1, 1943
    B. October 31, 1942
    C. December 7, 1941
    D. November 25, 1940

Multiple Choice Study Guide/Quiz Questions *Farewell to Manzanar*

Foreword, Chronology, and Terms, continued

8. When did evacuees begin to arrive at the Manzanar Camp?
   A. March 25, 1942
   B. January 1, 1940
   C. April 19, 1941
   D. July 4, 1940

9. What was the Supreme Court ruling of December 18, 1944?
   A. Anyone can be held in detention during wartime.
   B. All Japanese-Americans had to leave the country.
   C. The camps would remain open for six more years.
   D. Loyal citizens cannot be held in detention camps.

10. When did World War II end?
    A. June 30, 1946
    B. April 24, 1948
    C. August 14, 1945
    D. November 21, 1944

11. What did Public Law 414 do for the Japanese aliens?
    A. It gave them the right to leave the camps.
    B. It gave them the right to get a drivers' license.
    C. It gave them the right to become naturalized U. S. citizens.
    D. It gave them the right to sue the U. S. government for damages.

12. When was Public Law 414 passed?
    A. 1952
    B. 1945
    C. 1984
    D. 1973

Multiple Choice Study Guide/Quiz Questions *Farewell to Manzanar*

Part I: Chapters 1, 2, 3

1. What is the setting when the story opens?
    A. The wharf in Long Beach, California, in 1941.
    B. A house in Hiroshima, Japan, in 1875.
    C.. The Manzanar camp in 1983.
    D. The U. S. Capitol in 1964.

2. Why did the fishing boats return?
    A. They had been chased back by German U-boats.
    B. There was a severe storm and it was not safe to stay out.
    C. Several of the men were sick and had to be taken to the hospital.
    D. They heard on their radios that the Japanese had bombed Pearl Harbor.

3. True or False: The night Papa heard the news, he celebrated by singing the Japanese national anthem.
    A. True
    B. False

4. The FBI thought the Japanese fishermen might be ___.
    A. poisoning the fish they caught
    B. contacting Japanese ships off the west coast
    C. trying to leave the U. S. and sail back to Japan
    D. smuggling enemy soldiers into the United States

5. True or False: When Papa was arrested, he maintained his dignity.
    A. True
    B. False

6. On Terminal Island, Jeanne was afraid of ___.
    A. the American soldiers who guarded them
    B. the loud noises from the factories
    C. the other Japanese people
    D. the bugs in her house

7. Order 9066 authorizes the War Department to define military areas in the western states and to ____.
    A. make all able-bodied men join the armed forces
    B. move soldiers into peoples' homes to spy on them
    C. take over private companies to manufacture war supplies
    D. exclude anyone who might be considered a threat to the war effort

Multiple Choice Study Guide/Quiz Questions *Farewell to Manzanar*

Part I: Chapters 1, 2, 3, continued

8. When she was in Boyle Heights, it was the first time Jeanne had ever felt ____ from a Caucasian (her teacher).
    A. open hostility
    B. tremendous fear
    C. complete understanding
    D. unconditional friendship

9. What happened to the Wakatsuki family?
    A. They were sent back to their own home.
    B. They were relocated to the Manzanar camp.
    C. They were allowed to stay in Boyle Heights.
    D. They were sent to stay with an American family in New Jersey.

10. Which of the following does **not** describe the barracks?
    A. cracks in walls
    B. crowded
    C. dusty
    D. warm

Multiple Choice Study Guide/Quiz Questions *Farewell to Manzanar*

Part I: Chapters 4, 5, 6

1. The War Department turned one barracks in the camp into a/an ___. factory
    A. canning
    B. clothing
    C. automobile
    D. ammunition

2. At the camp, Jeanne continually had ____.
    A. a sore throat
    B. an ear infection
    C. a rash on her arms and legs
    D. stomach cramps and diarrhea

3. For Mama, using the ____ was a humiliation that she never got used to.
    A. latrines
    B. public well
    C. English language
    D. second-hand clothing

4. Jeanne described the situation as ____.
    A. a kick in the stomach
    B. a knife in the back
    C. a slap in the face
    D. a broken heart

5. According to Jeanne, which area of the camp caused her family to collapse as an integrated unit?
    A. school
    B. mess hall
    C. barracks
    D. Catholic church

6. Mama went to work at the camp as ____.
    A. a dietician
    B. a secretary
    C. an interpreter
    D. a seamstress

Multiple Choice Study Guide/Quiz Questions *Farewell to Manzanar*

Part I: Chapters 4, 5, 6, continued

7. How old is Jeanne in this part of the story?
    A. 15
    B. 10
    C. 7
    D. 2

8. True or False: When Jeanne first saw her father as he got off the bus at the camp, she cried.
    A. True
    B. False

9. As an adult, Jeanne compared her father's cane to ___.
    A. a crutch
    B. a baseball bat
    C. a samurai sword
    D. a diamond necklace

10. What job did Papa have at Fort Lincoln?
    A. auto mechanic
    B. radio operator
    C. prison guard
    D. interviewer

Multiple Choice Study Guide/Quiz Questions *Farewell to Manzanar*

Part I: Chapters 7, 8, 9, 10, 11

1. The interrogator asked Papa what he thought of the Japanese attack on Pearl Harbor. What was Papa's response?

    A. Papa said he thought the Japanese were fools for bombing the United States and he hoped that the U. S. bombed Japan back.
    B. Papa said he was sad for both countries; that the bombing and war were the things that happened when military men were in control.
    C. Papa said that the Japanese deserved to be world leaders and it was right for them to bomb other countries.
    D. Papa said the United States did not treat Japanese immigrants well so he was not surprised that the Japanese had attacked.

2. Some of the women in the camp accused Papa of being *inu*, which means ____.
    A. collaborator or informer
    B. racist or anti-Japanese
    C. violent soldier
    D. rebel

3. How was Papa's attack on Mama stopped?
    A. Mama escaped and hid in another barracks.
    B. The military police took Papa away.
    C. Kiyo punched Papa in the face.
    D. Papa passed out from drinking.

4. True or False: To a Japanese-American men who were held at Fort Lincoln, the charge of disloyalty was the greatest possible disgrace.
    A. True
    B. False

5. Fred Tayama was beaten because he ___.
    A. openly called for the Japanese to attack another American base
    B. had broken his engagement with one of the young women
    C. had stolen sugar from the kitchen and sold it for a profit
    D. was friendly with the camp administrators

6. What event occurred as a result of Fred's beating and the arrest of one of the suspects?
    A. a debate
    B. a riot
    C. a sit-in
    D. an early curfew

Multiple Choice Study Guide/Quiz Questions *Farewell to Manzanar*

Part I: Chapters 7, 8, 9, 10, 11, continued

7. Where was the Japanese-American crew when the MPs burst in on them?
    A. in a barracks
    B. in the kitchen of the mess hall
    C. in a shack near the reservoir
    D. in the camp's church

8. The second question on the Loyalty Oath asked the signers to do three things. Which of the following was not one of those things?
    A. forswear any allegiance to Japan
    B. defend the United States from attack
    C. swear unqualified allegiance to the United States
    D. change their first and last names to ones that sounded more "American"

9. What word did Jeanne use to describe the Loyalty Oath?
    A. silly
    B. grotesque
    C. infuriating
    D. appropriate

10. How did Papa answer the two questions on the Loyalty Oath?
    A. YES NO
    B. NO NO
    C. NO YES
    D. YES YES

Multiple Choice Study Guide/Quiz Questions *Farewell to Manzanar*

Part II: Chapters 12, 13, 14, 15

1. The word *manzanar* is Spanish. What is the English translation of the word?
    A. apple orchard
    B. fertile farmland
    C. guarded prison
    D. place for traitors

2. Jeanne said something near the camp symbolized "the turning of our life in the camp, from the outrageous to the tolerable." What was it?
    A. the river
    B. pear trees
    C. the mountains
    D. the change of the seasons

3. True or False: After the first year, the residents were allowed outside the wire for recreation.
    A. True
    B. False

4. Papa was doing several activities. Which of the following was not one of these activities?
    A. collecting driftwood
    B. painting watercolors
    C. making a rock garden
    D. learning to be an auto mechanic

5. True or False: The residents worked to make the camp look like an ancient Japanese village.
    A. True
    B. False

6. What did the residents do as the months turned into years?
    A. give up and sink into deep depression
    B. build a series of tunnels to try and escape
    C. create normalcy and keep anger under control
    D. openly rebel and make life difficult for the administration

7. What would Jeanne have done if she had been told she was free?
    A. run into the mountains
    B. go back to Long Beach
    C. move to the East Coast
    D. go right back to the camp

Multiple Choice Study Guide/Quiz Questions *Farewell to Manzanar*

Part II: Chapters 12, 13, 14, 15, continued

8. Jeanne described one activity as a "misuse of the body." What was this activity?
    A. ballet
    B. tennis
    C. swimming
    D. gymnastics

9. Jeanne wanted to do something but Papa refused to let her. What did she want to do?
    A. learn to drive a car
    B. have her first boyfriend
    C. get baptized and confirmed as a Catholic
    D. take lessons on how to be a proper Japanese woman

10. What happened to Woody?
    A. he was drafted into the U. S. Army
    B. he was sent to another camp
    C. he was sent back to Japan
    D. he got cancer

Multiple Choice Study Guide/Quiz Questions *Farewell to Manzanar*

Part II: Chapters 16, 17, 18, 19

1. In the first case involving the camps, the Supreme Court ruled that the army ____ impose a curfew and place restrictions on racial groups.
    A. could
    B. could not

2. In the second case involving the camps, the Supreme Court allowed the ____ of the Japanese.
    A. murder
    B. evacuation
    C. deportation
    D. reeducation

3. In the third case called Ex Parte Endo, the Supreme Court ruled that the government ____ have the right to imprison loyal citizens against their will.
    A. did
    B. did not

4. How did Jeanne feel when she thought about people hating her and her family?
    A. scared
    B. defiant
    C. furious
    D. humiliated

5. What comparison did Jeanne use to describe Papa now?
    A. like a slave freed after the Civil War
    B. like a little boy in a room full of new toys
    C. like a young man with his whole life ahead of him
    D. like an old man who could not walk without a cane

6. True or False: Papa immediately made plans to be the first family to leave the camp.
    A. True
    B. False

7. What caused the camps to be closed completely?
    A. The U.S. won the war.
    B. The Japanese revolted and freed themselves
    C. The U. S. ran out of money to pay for the camps.
    D. Other U. S. citizens protested and had the camps closed.

Multiple Choice Study Guide/Quiz Questions *Farewell to Manzanar*

Part II: Chapters 16, 17, 18, 19, continued

8. Where did Woody go in 1946 and why?
    A. He went to New York City to look for a new job.
    B. He went to Japan to visit his father's relatives.
    C. He went to Washington, D. C. to talk to the President.
    D. He went to Long Beach, California, to see their old neighbors.

9. Jeanne said the family left the camp "in style." How did they do this?
    A. They all wore new clothes.
    B. They organized a parade to march out of the camp.
    C. They decorated the bus with streamers and flowers.
    D. Papa bought a Nash sedan and the family drove away.

10. What did Mama and Papa do when they settled into Cabrillo Homes?
    A. Mama became a nurse and Papa went back to fishing.
    B. Mama became a dressmaker and Papa taught English to Japanese students.
    C. Mama worked at a fish cannery and Papa drafted plans for a housing cooperative.
    D. Mama worked as a nutritionist and Papa got a job as a maintenance man.

Multiple Choice Study Guide/Quiz Questions *Farewell to Manzanar*

Part II: Chapters 20, 21

1. What did Jeanne do on her first day in her new class that amazed one of the students?
    A. She twirled a baton.
    B. She did a Japanese dance.
    C. She read out loud in English.
    D. She lost her temper and yelled at the teacher.

2. What was Jeanne's double impulse?
    A. She wanted to be completely American and completely Japanese.
    B. She wanted to be smart but not compete with the boys.
    C. She wanted to disappear and be accepted.
    D. She wanted to date American boys but marry a Japanese boy.

3. True or False: Jeanne was often invited to the homes of the other girls.
    A. True
    B. False

4. How did Jeanne view her situation as it was happening?
    A. She thought the situation was her fault.
    B. She was infuriated.
    C. She blamed her parents.
    D. She did not care one way or the other.

5. What did Jeanne unconsciously learn from being chosen as a baton twirler by the Boy Scouts?
    A. The Girl Scouts were less prejudicial than the Boy Scouts.
    B. She was highly competitive and had to be the best at everything.
    C. She was able to use her sexuality and femininity to get accepted.
    D. If she had an American friend doors would open for her.

6. True or False: After Woody returned from Japan, Papa began to depend on him more instead of being in charge himself.
    A. True
    B. False

7. What happened when Jeanne and Radine went to high school?
    A. They traveled together in the same social circles.
    B. They both became dancers.
    C. Jeanne became a singer but Radine was not chosen.
    D. Jeanne felt demoralized watching Radine's success.

Multiple Choice Study Guide/Quiz Questions *Farewell to Manzanar*

Part II: Chapters 20, 21, continued

8. Who was in the dream that Jeanne had several times?
    A. a Japanese princess
    B. a blond, blue-eyed high school girl
    C. her mother as a teenager
    D. Jeanne as she looked then

9. During her senior year, Jeanne was elected _____.
    A. president of the student body
    B. lead baton twirler in the drill team
    C. carnival queen
    D. editor of the school yearbook

10. What did Jeanne's dress look like?
    A. form-fitting and strapless
    B. a short, flowered sarong
    C. a Japanese kimono
    D. high neck, full skirt, ruffles

Multiple Choice Study Guide/Quiz Questions *Farewell to Manzanar*

Part III: Chapter 22
1. How long did it take Jeanne to get the confidence to deal with Manzanar?
 A. 20 years
 B. 3 years
 C. 35 years
 D. 11 years

2. What family "firsts" did Jeanne accomplish?
 A. first to speak fluent English;, first to get a high-paying job
 B. first to marry out of her race; first to finish college
 C. first to go to the East Coast; first to have children
 D. first to forget about their ordeal; first to forgive the US administration

3. Who went to the Manzanar site with Jeanne?
 A. her parents
 B. her brothers
 C. her husband and children
 D. her editor and publisher

4. True or False: The camp looked exactly as it had looked when she was there.
 A. True
 B. False

5. The title of Chapter 22 indicates that Jeanne heard _____ at the camp.
 A. the sound of the sirens during the riot
 B. the wind in the apple trees
 C. the sound of bombs exploding
 D. ten thousand voices

6. How did Jeanne try to look at the area?
 A. as a memorial not to engage in prejudice
 B. as a historical and archaeological site
 C. as a bad time that she managed to get over
 D. as her worst nightmares

7. What inscription was on the flagpole circle?
 A. BUILT BY WADA AND CREW, JUNE 10, 1942 AD
 B. JAPANESE GO HOME
 C. RESIDNENCE OF THE WAKATSUKI FAMILY
 D. REST IN PEACE TO ALL WHO DIED HERE

Multiple Choice Study Guide/Quiz Questions *Farewell to Manzanar*

Part III: Chapter 22, continued

8. Jeanne's oldest daughter was ____, the same age as Jeanne when the camp closed.
    A. 7
    B. 19
    C. 14
    D. 11

9. True or False: The trip helped Jeanne forget all about her experience at Manzanar.
    A. True
    B. False

10. Jeanne remembered that leaving the camp in the car was _____.
    A. like a second honeymoon to her parents
    B. her father's last act of defiance
    C. considered a put-down by those who could not afford a car
    D. a fun and exciting trip

ANSWER SHEET MULTIPLE CHOICE STUDY/QUIZ QUESTIONS
Farewell to Manzanar

Part I: Foreword, Chronology, Terms	**Part I: Chapters 1, 2, 3**	**Part I: Chapters 4, 5, 6.**	**Part I: Chapters 7, 8, 9, 10, 11**
1.	1.	1.	1.
2.	2.	2.	2.
3.	3.	3.	3.
4.	4.	4.	4.
5.	5.	5.	5.
6.	6.	6.	6.
7.	7.	7.	7.
8.	8.	8.	8.
9.	9.	9.	9.
10.	10.	10.	10.

Part II: Chapters 12, 13, 14, 15.	**Part II: Chapters 16, 17, 18, 19.**	**Part II: Chapters 20, 21.**	**Part III: Chapter 22**
1.	1.	1.	1.
2.	2.	2.	2.
3.	3.	3.	3.
4.	4.	4.	4.
5.	5.	5.	5.
6.	6.	6.	6.
7.	7.	7.	7.
8.	8.	8.	8.
9.	9.	9.	9.
10.	10.	10.	10.

ANSWER SHEET KEY MULTIPLE CHOICE STUDY/QUIZ QUESTIONS
Farewell to Manzanar

Part I: Foreword, Chronology, Terms	**Part I: Chapters 1, 2, 3**	**Part I: Chapters 4, 5, 6**	**Part I: Chapters 7, 8, 9, 10, 11**
1. D	1. A	1. B	1. B
2. B	2. D	2. D	2. A
3. C	3. B False	3. A	3. C
4. A	4. B	4. C	4. A True
5. B False	5. A True	5. B	5. D
6. B	6. C	6. A	6. B
7. C	7. D	7. C	7. C
8. A	8. A	8. A	8. D
9. D	9. B	9. C	9. B
10. A	10. D	10. D	10. D

Part II: Chapters 12, 13, 14, 15	**Part II: Chapters 16, 17, 18, 19**	**Part II: Chapters 20, 21**	**Part III: Chapter 22**
1. A	1. A	1. C	1. A
2. B	2. B	2. C	2. B
3. A True	3. B	3. B False	3. C
4. D	4. D	4. A	4. B False
5. B False	5. A	5. C	5. D
6. C	6. B False	6. A True	6. B
7. D	7. A	7. D	7. A
8. A	8. B	8. B	8. C
9. C	9. D	9. C	9. B False
10. A	10. C	10. D	10. B

PREREADING VOCABULARY WORKSHEETS

Prereading Vocabulary Worksheets *Farewell to Manzanar*

Foreword, Chronology, Terms
Part I: Using Prior Knowledge and Contextual Clues
Below are the sentences in which the vocabulary words appear in the text. Read the sentence. Use any clues you can find in the sentence combined with your prior knowledge, and write what you think the italicized words mean in the space provided.

1. When we first considered writing a book about the internment of Japanese Americans during World war Two, we told a New York writer friend about the idea.

_____

2. He said, "It's a dead issue. These days you can hardly get people to read about live issues."

_____

3. As the photos brought that world back, I began to dredge up feelings that had lain submerged since the forties.

_____

4. Writing it has been a way of coming to terms with the impact these years have had on my entire life.

_____

5. U. S. Congress grants naturalization rights to free whites and people of African descent, omitting mention of Oriental races.

_____

6. The Japanese government lifts its ban on emigration, allowing its citizens for the first time to make permanent moves to other countries.

_____

7. Alien Land Bill prevents Japanese aliens from owning land in California.

_____

8. Issei. The first generation. The Issei were born in Japan.

_____

Prereading Vocabulary Worksheets *Farewell to Manzanar*

Foreword, Chronology, Terms

Part 1, continued

9. Nisei. The second generation, the children of the Issei. American citizens by birth, almost all Nisei were born before the Second World War.

_____

10. Sansei. The third generation of American with Japanese ancestry, most of them born during or after the Second World War.

Part II: Determining the Meaning: Match the vocabulary words to their dictionary definitions.

_____ 1. internment	A. admitted to citizenship
_____ 2. issue	B. matter or point of discussion
_____ 3. dredge	C. third generation; born in US after WWII
_____ 4. impact	D. non-citizens living in a country
_____ 5. naturalization	E. being forced to stay in a place
_____ 6. emigration	F. second generation; born in US before WWII
_____ 7. aliens	G. forceful effect
_____ 8. Issei	H. bring up
_____ 9. Nisei	I. first generation; born in Japan
_____ 10. Sansei	J. resettling in another country

Prereading Vocabulary Worksheets *Farewell to Manzanar*

Part I: Chapters 1, 2, 3
Part I: Using Prior Knowledge and Contextual Clues
Below are the sentences in which the vocabulary words appear in the text. Read the sentence. Use any clues you can find in the sentence combined with your prior knowledge, and write what you think the italicized words mean in the space provided.

1. It was a kind of duty, perhaps away of adding a little good luck to the voyage or warding off the bad.

_____

2. We watched until the boats became a row of tiny white gulls on the horizon. Our vigil would end when they slipped over the edge and disappeared.

_____

3. He burned a lot of papers, too, anything that might suggest he still had some connections with Japan. These precautions didn't do him much good.

_____

4. To the FBI every radio owner was a potential saboteur.

_____

5. The confiscators were often deputies sworn in hastily during the turbulent days right after Pearl Harbor . . .

_____

6. The confiscators were often deputies sworn in hastily during the turbulent days right after Pearl Harbor.

_____

7. Papa had been the patriarch. He had always decided everything in the family.

_____

Prereading Vocabulary Worksheets *Farewell to Manzanar*

Part I: Chapters 1, 2, 3

Part 1, continued

8. These were mainly days of quiet, desperate waiting for what seemed at the time to be <u>inevitable.</u>

_____

9. I could see a few tents set up, the first rows of black <u>barracks,</u> and beyond them, blurred by sand, rows of barracks that seemed to spread for miles across this plain.

_____

10. We could hear voices in other <u>cubicles</u> now.

_____

Part II: Determining the Meaning: Match the vocabulary words to their dictionary definitions.

_____ 1. warding   A. watching

_____ 2. vigil   B. very small rooms

_____ 3. precautions   C. unavoidable

_____ 4. saboteur   D. authorities who take and keep things

_____ 5. confiscators   E. large, plain building where many people live

_____ 6. turbulent   F. keeping away

_____ 7. patriarch   G. male head of the family

_____ 8. inevitable   H. care taken beforehand

_____ 9. barracks   I. person who harms an enemy nation

_____ 10. cubicles   J. violent

Prereading Vocabulary Worksheets *Farewell to Manzanar*

Part I: Chapters 4, 5, 6
Part I: Using Prior Knowledge and Contextual Clues
Below are the sentences in which the vocabulary words appear in the text. Read the sentence. Use any clues you can find in the sentence combined with your prior knowledge, and write what you think the italicized words mean in the space provided.

1. They began to issue military surplus from the First World War- olive drab knit caps, earmuffs, peacoats, canvas leggings.

    _____

2. It seems comical, looking back; we were a band of Charlie Chaplins* marooned in the California desert.

    _____

3. But at the time, it was pure chaos.

    _____

4. The sink was a long metal trough against one wall, with a row of spigots for hot and cold water.

    _____

5. They made some recommendations, and edicts went out that families *must* start eating together again.

    _____

6. Whatever dignity or feeling of filial strength we may have known before December 1941 was lost, and we did not recover it until many years after the war . . . .

    _____

7. Whatever He Did Had Flourish

    _____

Prereading Vocabulary Worksheets *Farewell to Manzanar*

Part I: Chapters 4, 5, 6

8. Japan was in the throes of that rapid, confusing <u>metamorphosis</u> from a feudal to an industrial nation, which began when Commodore Perry's black-hulled armada steamed into Tokyo Bay and forced the Japanese to open their ports and cities to western trade.

_____

9. In those days he was a headstrong <u>idealist</u>.

_____

10. Then he set the cleaver down, stepped back, reached behind him without looking for a towel one of my sisters somehow had there waiting, and as he wiped his hands he said <u>imperiously</u> to his sons, "Cut it up. You girls, bring the platters here. Everybody wants to eat."

_____

* **Charlie Chaplin** *was a star of the silent movies from around 1917-1939. His most famous character, The Little Tramp, dressed in a raggedy suit and wobbled along carrying a cane.*

Part II: Determining the Meaning: Match the vocabulary words to their dictionary definitions.

_____ 1. surplus   A. a showy display

_____ 2. marooned   B. change of form or structure

_____ 3. chaos   C. narrow, open container that holds water

_____ 4. trough   D. rules proclaimed by one in authority

_____ 5. edicts   E. person who wants things to be perfect

_____ 6. filial   F. great confusion or disorder

_____ 7. flourish   G. in an arrogant, domineering way

_____ 8. metamorphosis   H. left in a helpless position

_____ 9. idealist   I. of a son or daughter

_____ 10. imperiously   J. extra

Prereading Vocabulary Worksheets *Farewell to Manzanar*

Part I: Chapters 7, 8, 9, 10, 11
Part I: Using Prior Knowledge and Contextual Clues
Below are the sentences in which the vocabulary words appear in the text. Read the sentence. Use any clues you can find in the sentence combined with your prior knowledge, and write what you think the italicized words mean in the space provided.

1. Years later I learned that *inu* also meant collaborator or informer.

   _____

2. He kept pursuing oblivion through drink, he kept abusing Mama, and there seemed to be no way out of it for anyone.

   _____

3. And it was the humiliation. It brought him face to face with his own vulnerability, his own powerlessness.

   _____

4. A vigilante party searched the corridors. When they failed to find their man, this half of the crowd moved off in search of others on their "death list."

   _____

5. What I recall vividly are the bells that began to toll late that night. After dispersing, some of the demonstrators organized shifts, and kept them tolling all over camp.

   _____

6. My brother-in-law Kaz was foreman of a reservoir maintenance detail, the only crew permitted to work or leave the camp limits the night of the riot.

   _____

7. Will you swear unqualified allegiance to the united States of America and faithfully defend the United States from any or all attack by foreign or domestic forces . . . .

   _____

Prereading Vocabulary Worksheets *Farewell to Manzanar*

Part I: Chapters 7, 8, 9, 10, 11

8. This part of it would have been comical if the results were not so grotesque. No self-respecting espionage agent would willingly admit he was disloyal.

_____

9. Now, outside in the dirt, Papa had him by the throat and would have strangled him, but some other men pulled them apart. I had never seen him so livid, yelling and out of his head with rage.

_____

10. It is a patriotic song that can also be read as a proverb, as a personal credo for endurance.

_____

Part II: Determining the Meaning: Match the vocabulary words to their dictionary definitions.

_____ 1. collaborator   A. being open to attack or injury

_____ 2. oblivion   B. ridiculous; absurd

_____ 3. vulnerability   C. someone who works with the enemy

_____ 4. vigilante   D. place where water is collected and stored

_____ 5. dispersing   E. extremely angry

_____ 6. reservoir   F. going away in different directions

_____ 7. unqualified   G. beliefs

_____ 8. grotesque   H. condition of being entirely forgotten

_____ 9. livid   I. someone who takes the law into their own hands

_____ 10. credo   J. complete; without limits or restrictions

Prereading Vocabulary Worksheets *Farewell to Manzanar*

Part II: Chapters 12, 13, 14, 15
Part I: Using Prior Knowledge and Contextual Clues
Below are the sentences in which the vocabulary words appear in the text. Read the sentence. Use any clues you can find in the sentence combined with your prior knowledge, and write what you think the italicized words mean in the space provided.

1. For all the pain it caused, the loyalty oath finally did speed up the relocation program. One result was a gradual easing of the congestion in the barracks.

2. Once the first year's turmoil cooled down, the authorities started letting us outside the wire for recreation.

3. Whitney reminded Papa of Fujiyama, that is, it gave him the same kind of spiritual sustenance. The tremendous beauty of those peaks was inspirational, as so many natural forms are to the Japanese. . . .

4. Subdued, resigned, Papa's life–all our lives–took on a pattern that would hold for the duration of the war.

5. Subdued, resigned, Papa's life–all our lives–took on a pattern that would hold for the duration of the war.

6. Camp One was about as far as I cared to venture. What's more, Block 28 was "where I lived" now. One night was plenty, one night every once in a while, to explore whatever was out there.

7. Two of my sisters had borne children there. They had both hemorrhaged badly, and blood plasma was in short supply, our needs being low on the wartime priority list.

Prereading Vocabulary Worksheets *Farewell to Manzanar*

Part II: Chapters 12, 13, 14, 15

8. Our family had begun to <u>dwindle</u>, along with the entire camp population. By the end of 1944 about 6,000 people remained, and those, for the most part, were the aging and the young.

_____

9. Climbing aboard he must have been thinking of those things, while Mama, no doubt, was thinking of the mother at Manzanar who had already received a <u>posthumous</u> Congressional Medal of honor on behalf of her son who'd been killed in Italy.

_____

10. Families were being torn <u>asunder</u> and those left behind knew no more about their own fate than they did of the loved ones moving on.

_____

(not tested)
She was a <u>Quaker</u>, like so many of the <u>Caucasians</u> who came in to teach and do volunteer work.
A <u>Quaker</u> is a member of a Christian group called The Society of Friends. The Quakers are generally opposed to war. A <u>Caucasian</u> is a member of the racial group from the original inhabitants of Europe, southwestern Asia, and northern Africa and their descendants all over the world.

Part II: Determining the Meaning: Match the vocabulary words to their dictionary definitions.

_____ 1. congestion   A. accepting what comes without complaint

_____ 2. turmoil   B. overcome by force; conquered

_____ 3. sustenance   C. dare to go

_____ 4. subdued   D. happening after death

_____ 5. resigned   E. coming in order of importance

_____ 6. venture   F. in pieces or separate parts

_____ 7. priority   G. an overcrowded condition

_____ 8. dwindle   H. make or become smaller

_____ 9. posthumous   I. nourishment or support

_____ 10. asunder   J. state of agitation or disturbance

Prereading Vocabulary Worksheets *Farewell to Manzanar*

Part II: Chapters 16, 17, 18, 19
Part I: Using Prior Knowledge and Contextual Clues
Below are the sentences in which the vocabulary words appear in the text. Read the sentence. Use any clues you can find in the sentence combined with your prior knowledge, and write what you think the italicized words mean in the space provided.

1. He challenged the racial bias of these actions and the abuse of his civil rights.

_____

2. Accepting this ruling, the army's Western Defense Command had already announced that the mass exclusion orders of 1942 were being rescinded.

_____

3. In addition to the traditionally racist organizations like the American Legion and The Native Sons of the Golden West, who had been agitating against the west coast Japanese for decades, new groups had sprung up during the war . . . .

_____

4. Before the war one of the standard charges against the Japanese was their clannishness, their standoffishness, their refusal to assimilate. The camps had made this a reality in the extreme.

_____

5. I would listen to the stories and I would cringe.

_____

6. Ominous reports of their reception began trickling back, to confirm our deepest fears.

_____

7. Just a hint of embarrassment gave them away, a tinge in the cheek for the fact that such a common item should now be so highly prized.

_____

Prereading Vocabulary Worksheets *Farewell to Manzanar*

Part II: Chapters 16, 17, 18, 19

8. When he's finally standing there, Woody is amazed at how his stance resembles Toyo's.
_____

9. A few days before we left manzanar Papa decided that since we had to go, we might as well leave in style, and by our own volition.
_____

10. That dread was gone. But those premonitions proved correct, in a way I hadn't been at all prepared for, on the first day back in public school, when the shape of what I truly had to deal with appeared to me for the first time.
_____

Part II: Determining the Meaning: Match the vocabulary words to their dictionary definitions.

_____ 1. bias   A. warnings of what is to come

_____ 2. rescinded   B. arousing public awareness and feeling

_____ 3. agitating   C. manner of standing

_____ 4. assimilate   D. unfavorable, threatening

_____ 5. cringe   E. preference based on prejudice

_____ 6. ominous   F. become like the others in custom, etc.

_____ 7. tinge   G. decision or choice

_____ 8. stance   H. canceled

_____ 9. volition   I. a slight coloring

_____ 10. premonitions   J. crouch in fear

Prereading Vocabulary Worksheets *Farewell to Manzanar*

Part II: Chapters 20, 21
Part I: Using Prior Knowledge and Contextual Clues
Below are the sentences in which the vocabulary words appear in the text. Read the sentence. Use any clues you can find in the sentence combined with your prior knowledge, and write what you think the italicized words mean in the space provided.

1. She was a warm, benevolent woman who tried to make this first day as easy as possible.

   _____

2. I wouldn't be faced with physical attack, or with overt shows of hatred.

   _____

3. This girl's guileless remark came as an illumination, an instant knowledge that brought with it the first buds of true shame.

   _____

4. You cannot deport 110,000 people unless you have stopped seeing individuals. Of course, for such a thing to happen, there has to be a kind of acquiescence on the part of the victims, some submerged belief that this treatment is deserved . . . .

   _____

5. At the same time I wondered why my citizenship had to be so loudly affirmed, and I couldn't imagine why affirming it would really make any difference.

   _____

6. This was exactly what I wanted. It also gave me the first sure sign of how certain intangible barriers might be crossed.

   _____

7. Yet while Woody grew, Papa seemed to shrink, losing potency.

   _____

Prereading Vocabulary Worksheets *Farewell to Manzanar*

Part II: Chapters 20, 21

8. I was ready to capitulate without a groan.
_____

9. Yet in that glare I sometimes detected a flicker of approval, as if this streak of independence, this refusal to be shaped by him reflected his own obstinance.
_____

10. "The high *neck*," she explained, studying my dress. "You look so . . . *sedate*. Just perfect for a queen."
_____

Part II: Determining the Meaning: Match the vocabulary words to their dictionary definitions.

_____ 1. benevolent   A. stubbornness

_____ 2. overt   B. agreement without objections

_____ 3. guileless   C. kindly, charitable

_____ 4. acquiescence   D. surrender on certain conditions

_____ 5. affirmed   E. declared to be true

_____ 6. intangible   F. public; not hidden

_____ 7. potency   G. power; strength

_____ 8. capitulate   H. calm; serious

_____ 9. obstinance   I. honest; straightforward

_____ 10. sedate   J. not able to be seen or touched

Prereading Vocabulary Worksheets *Farewell to Manzanar*

Part III: Chapter 23
Part I: Using Prior Knowledge and Contextual Clues
Below are the sentences in which the vocabulary words appear in the text. Read the sentence. Use any clues you can find in the sentence combined with your prior knowledge, and write what you think the italicized words mean in the space provided.

1. By the age of seventeen I know that making it, in the terms I had tried to adopt, was not only unlikely, but false and empty, no more authentic for me than trying to emulate my Great-aunt Toyo.

   _____

2. By the age of seventeen I know that making it, in the terms I had tried to adopt, was not only unlikely, but false and empty, no more authentic for me than trying to emulate my Great-aunt Toyo.

   _____

3. This time it was not the pain of memory. It was simply her validation that all those things had taken place.

   _____

4. About a half a mile in we spotted a white obelisk gleaming in the distance and marking a subtle line where the plain begins gradually to slope upward . . . .

   _____

5. For a moment I was strolling again, finding childish comfort in its incongruous design.

   _____

6. The orange peels would smolder in there, and the men would hunker down around the cans and watch the smoke seep out the holes.

   _____

7. Mama had been packing, and that brought the uncertainty of our future to such a sharp point, her back went into spasms.

   _____

Prereading Vocabulary Worksheets *Farewell to Manzanar*

Part III: Chapter 23

8. Chizu was the <u>placator</u> now, leaning forward from the back to pat him on the shoulder.

_____

9. He wouldn't listen and told us to hold on, while he swung into the street, <u>careening</u> past emptying barracks where suitcases and duffel bags sat stacked.

_____

10. We came to a firebreak and Papa plunged into it, began to cut a twisty path across its emptiness, shouting, "Hyah! Hyah!," <u>gouging</u> ragged tracks through the dusty sand.

_____

Part II: Determining the Meaning: Match the vocabulary words to their dictionary definitions.

_____ 1. authentic   A. peacemaker

_____ 2. emulate   B. digging; tearing out

_____ 3. validation   C. confirmation; support by facts

_____ 4. obelisk   D. involuntary muscle contraction

_____ 5. incongruous   E. out of place

_____ 6. hunker   F. rushing headlong with a swaying motion

_____ 7. spasm   G. a tapering, four-sided structure with a pyramid shaped top

_____ 8. placator   H. imitate; act like

_____ 9. careening   I. squat; sit back on ones heels

_____ 10. gouging   J. real; genuine

ANSWER KEY - VOCABULARY *Farewell to Manzanar*

Foreword, Chronology, Terms	Part I: Chapters 1, 2, 3	Part I: Chapters 4, 5, 6
1. E	1. F	1. J
2. B	2. A	2. H
3. H	3. H	3. F
4. G	4. I	4. C
5. A	5. D	5. D
6. J	6. J	6. I
7. D	7. G	7. A
8. I	8. C	8. B
9. F	9. E	9. E
10. C	10. B	10. G

Part I: Chapters 7-11	Part II: Chapters 12-15	Part II: Chapters 16-19
1. C	1. G	1. E
2. H	2. J	2. H
3. A	3. I	3. B
4. I	4. B	4. F
5. F	5. A	5. J
6. D	6. C	6. D
7. J	7. E	7. I
8. B	8. H	8. C
9. E	9. D	9. G
10. G	10. F	10. A

Part II: Chapters 20, 21	Part III: Chapter 22
1. C	1. J
2. F	2. H
3. I	3. C
4. B	4. G
5. E	5. E
6. J	6. I
7. G	7. D
8. D	8. A
9. A	9. F
10. H	10. B

DAILY LESSON PLANS

LESSON ONE

Objectives
    1. To introduce the *Farewell to Manzanar* unit
    2. To relate prior knowledge to the new material
    3. To receive books and other related materials (study guides, reading assignment)
    4. To do the prereading work for the Foreword, Chronology, and Terms

Activity #1
    Show students some pictures of the Manzanar relocation camp or the other relocation camps, as well as the Long Beach area of California from the early 1940's (World War II era.) Tell students they are going to read book about the experiences of one woman who lived at the Manzanar camp for several years. Explain that the book is her memoir of those years. It is written in the first person, told from Jeanne's point of view as a young child, with some of her observations as an adult looking back also included. Discuss with students why someone would want to write such a book. Ask students how they think they will benefit from reading the book.

Activity #2
    Ask students to tell you what they know about World War II in general, the situation the Japanese Americans faced during the war, Jeanne Wakatsuki Houston, and the book. Do a group KWL with students. The form is included in this unit plan. Put any information the students know in the K column (What I Know.) Ask students what they want to find out and put those questions in the W column (What I Want to Find Out.) Keep the KWL sheet and refer back to it while reading. After reading the novel, complete the L column (What I Learned.)

Activity #3
    Distribute the materials students will use in this unit. Explain in detail how students are to use these materials.
    <u>Study Guides</u> Students should preview the study guide questions before each reading assignment to get a feeling for what events and ideas are important in that section. After reading the section, students will (as a class or individually) answer the questions to review the important events and ideas from that section of the book. Students should keep the study guides as study materials for the unit test.

    <u>Reading / Writing Assignment Sheet</u> You (the teachers) need to fill in the reading and writing assignment sheet to let students know when their reading has to be completed. You can either write the assignment sheet on a side blackboard or bulletin board and leave it there for students to see each day, or you can duplicate copies for each student to have. In either case, you should advise students to become very familiar with the reading assignments so they know what is expected of them.

Daily Lesson Plans *Farewell to Manzanar*

LESSON ONE, continued

    Unit Outline You may find it helpful to distribute copies of the Unit Outline to your students so they can keep track of upcoming lessons and assignments. You may also want to post a copy of the Unit Outline on a bulletin board and cross off each lesson as you complete it.

    Extra Activities Center The Extra Activities Packet portion of this unit contains suggestions for a library of related books and articles in your classroom as well as crossword and word search puzzles. Make an extra activities center in your room where you will keep these materials for students to use. Bring the books and articles in from the library and keep several copies of the puzzles on hand. Explain to students that these materials are available for students to use when they finish reading assignments or other class work early.

    Books Each school has its own rules and regulations regarding student use of school books. Advise students of the procedures that are normal for your school.

    Notebook or Unit Folder You may want the students to keep all of their worksheets, notes, and other papers for the unit together in a binder or notebook. During the first class meeting, tell them how you want them to arrange the folder. Make divider pages for vocabulary worksheets, prereading study guide questions, review activities, notes, and tests. You may want to give a grade for accuracy in keeping the folder.

Activity #4

    Show students how to preview the study questions and do the vocabulary work for the Foreword, Chronology, and Terms of *Farewell to Manzanar*. If students do not finish this assignment in class, they should complete it prior to the next class meeting.

KWL
Farewell to Manzanar

Directions: Before reading, think about what you already know about *Farewell to Manzanar* and/or Jeanne Wakatsuki Houston. Write the information in the **K** column. Think about what you would like to find out from reading the book. Write your questions in the **W** column. After you have read the book, use the **L** column to write the answers to your questions from the W column, and anything else you remember from the book.

What I KNOW	What I WANT to Learn	What I LEARNED

Daily Lesson Plans *Farewell to Manzanar*

LESSON TWO

Objectives
1. To read the Foreword, Chronology, and Terms
2. To review the main ideas and events from the Foreword, Chronology, and Terms
3. To become acquainted with the Nonficiton reading assignment.

Activity #1

You may want to read the Foreword aloud to the students to set the mood for the novel. Invite willing students to read the Chronology and Terms aloud to the rest of the class. Discuss with students why it is important that they have a sense of the history of Japanese immigration to the United States, the events that led up to the internment, and the related court rulings. Remind students that they should refer back to these pages if they have difficulty keeping the sequence of events straight.

Activity #2

Give the students time to answer the study guide questions, and then discuss the answers in detail. Write the answers on the board or overhead projector film so students can have the correct answers for study purposes. Encourage students to take notes. If the students own their books, encourage them to use highlighters or colored pens to mark important passages and the answers to the study guide questions.

Note: it is a good practice in public speaking and leadership skills for individual students to take charge of leading the discussion of the study questions. Perhaps a different student could go to the front of the class and lead the discussion each day that they study questions are discussed during the unit. Of course, the teacher should guide the discussion when appropriate and be sure to fill in any gaps the students leave.

Activity #3

Distribute copies of the Nonfiction Assignment sheet and go over it in detail with the students. Explain to students that they each are to read at least one nonfiction piece at some time during the unit. This could be a book, a magazine article, or information from an encyclopedia or the Internet. Students will fill out a nonfiction assignment sheet after completing the reading to help you (the teacher) evaluate their reading experiences and to help the students think about and evaluate their own reading experiences. Give them the due date for the assignment (Lesson 19.)

Encourage students to read about topics that are related to the theme of the novel. Some suggested books are:
- Cooper, Michael. *Remembering Manzanar.*
- Harvey, Robert. *Amanche: The Story of Japanese Internment in Colorado During World War II.*
- Robinson, Gerald. *Elusive Truth: Four Photographers at Manzanar.*
- Stanley, Jerry. *I Am an American: A True Story of Japanese Internment.*

Daily Lesson Plans *Farewell to Manzanar*

LESSON TWO, continued

Students may want to look at Web sites such as the following:
- Children of the Camps/INTERNMENT SITES
    http://www.children-of-the-camps.org/resources/internment.html
- Manzanar National Historic Site (National Park Service)
    http://www.nps.gov/manz/

LESSON THREE

Objectives
1. To do the prereading work for Part I: Chapters 1, 2, 3
2. To read Part I: Chapters 1, 2, 3
3. To practice reading orally
4. To have students' oral reading evaluated
5. To review the main ideas and events from Part I: Chapters 1, 2, 3

Activity #1
Give students ten or fifteen minutes to complete the prereading vocabulary worksheet and preview the study guide questions.

Activity #2
Tell students their oral reading ability will be evaluated. Show them copies of the Oral Reading Evaluation Form and discuss it. Model correct intonation and expression by reading the first few paragraphs of Chapter 1 aloud.

Activity #3
Call on individual students to read a few paragraphs aloud. Encourage the other students to follow along silently in their books. If you have a student who is unwilling or unable to read in front of the group make arrangements to do his or her evaluation privately at another time. Mark the oral reading evaluation forms as the students read. If all students have read orally before the chapters have been completed, assign the remainder of the text as individual silent reading.

Activity #4
Write the study questions on the board or on a piece of chart paper. Work with the whole class to answer the questions.

NONFICTION ASSIGNMENT SHEET - *Farewell to Manzanar*
(To be completed after reading the required nonfiction article)

Name _____ Date _____ Class _____

Title of Nonfiction Read _____

Written By _____ Publication Date _____

Web Site Address (if applicable) _____

I. Factual Summary: Write a short summary of the piece you read.

II. Vocabulary:
    1. Which vocabulary words were difficult?

    2. What did you do to help yourself understand the words?

III. Interpretation: What was the main point the author wanted you to get from reading his/her work?

IV. Criticism:
    1. Which points of the piece did you agree with or find easy to believe? Why?

    2. With which points of the piece did you disagree or find difficult to believe? Why?

V. Personal Response:
    1. What do you think about this piece?

    2. How does this piece help you better understand the novel *Farewell to Manzanar*?

ORAL READING EVALUATION *Farewell to Manzanar*

Name _____ Class _____ Date _____

SKILL	EXCELLENT	GOOD	AVERAGE	FAIR	POOR
FLUENCY	5	4	3	2	1
CLARITY	5	4	3	2	1
AUDIBILITY	5	4	3	2	1
PRONUNCIATION	5	4	3	2	1
_____	5	4	3	2	1
_____	5	4	3	2	1

TOTAL _____ GRADE _____

COMMENTS:

Daily Lesson Plans *Farewell to Manzanar*

LESSON FOUR

<u>Objectives</u>
1. To do the prereading work for Part I: Chapters 4, 5, 6
2. To read Part I: Chapters 4, 5, 6
3. To review the main ideas and events in Part I: Chapters 4, 5, 6
4. To begin to identify examples of character traits

<u>Activity #1</u>
Have partners preview the study questions and complete the vocabulary work together.

<u>Activity #2</u>
Have students work with the same partner to read the chapters. Tell them to take turns reading aloud. Suggest that they stop after a few pages to orally summarize what they have read, and to answer the pertinent study questions.

<u>Activity #3</u>
Review the study guide questions and answers with students. Then have students work with their partners to write a few additional questions about the chapters. Have each pair read their questions aloud and let them call on students to answer the questions.

<u>Activity #4 Minilesson: Character Traits</u>
Explain that in a nonfiction memoir such as *Farewell to Manzanar*, the author acquaints the reader with the people involved by describing character traits such as physical attributes, thoughts, and feelings. Words to describe character traits include *strong, weak, polite, rude, selfish, selfless, prejudiced,* and *open-minded*. The author develops these traits by telling what the people say, do, and think. Remind students that in this book, Jeanne Wakatsuki Houston is describing real people. She portrays them as she remembers them. Her portrayals are influenced by her own perceptions of the events and people. She gives more detail about Mama and Papa than she does about most of her other family members, but the reader can still learn something about all of these people through the author's descriptions.

Have students look for the character traits of both Mama and Papa as they read. Distribute copies of the Character Trait Chart (included.) Ask students to fill in what they have learned about Mama and Papa so far. Tell them they should continue to be aware the character traits of both characters as they read, and that they will continue the discussion and complete more of the chart during Lesson 17. As an extension, students can copy the character traits chart and use it to write about other people in the book, including Jeanne herself.

CHARACTER TRAITS CHART *Farewell to Manzanar*

Directions: Fill in the charts for Mama and Papa with examples from the novel.

Mama's Character Traits	Words, Thoughts, or Actions That Illustrate the Trait
1.	
2.	
3.	

Papa's Character Traits	Words, Thoughts, or Actions That Illustrate the Trait
1.	
2.	
3.	

Daily Lesson Plans *Farewell to Manzanar*

LESSON FIVE

Objectives
1. To write to inform
2. To have a piece of writing evaluated by the teacher

Activity #1

Distribute Writing Assignment #1 and discuss the directions in detail. Allow the remaining class time for students to work on the assignment. Give students an additional two or three class periods to complete the assignment if necessary.

Activity #2

Distribute copies of the Writing Evaluation Form (included in this Unit Plan.) Explain to the students that during Lesson Nine you will be holding individual writing conferences about this writing assignment. Make sure they are familiar with the criteria on the Writing Evaluation Form.

Follow-Up: After you have graded the assignments, have a writing conference with each student. (This Unit Plan schedules one in Lesson Nine.) After the writing conference, allow students to revise their papers using your suggestions to complete the revisions. You may want to grade the revisions on an A-C-E scale, (all revisions well done, some revisions made, few or no revisions made.) This will speed the grading time and still give some credit for the students' efforts.

Publication: You may want to publish students' newspaper articles by putting them on a bulletin board. Also consider creating a class newspaper where students can contribute their articles. Posting the articles on the class Web site is also another means of publication.

WRITING ASSIGNMENT 1 *Farewell to Manzanar*
Writing to Inform

PROMPT

In the first few chapters of *Farewell to Manzanar* you read about the U. S. government's efforts to relocate thousands of Japanese-Americans living along the west coast to inland camps. Now you will take on the persona of a newspaper journalist in 1942 writing a news article about the event.

PREWRITING

A newspaper article tells *who, what, when, where,* and *why,* about a topic as well as *how* it happened. Write these six words in a column on a piece of paper. Next to each word, write as much information as you can that is related to the move to Manzanar or the other camps. You may need to do some extra research to complete this step of the writing assignment.

DRAFTING

First, write a headline for your news article. The headline should only be a few words; it does not need to be a complete sentence. Get your main idea across in the headline. Then write the article. Your lead sentence in the first paragraph should tell what happened, when it happened, and who was involved. The rest of the article should fill in more of the details. If possible, use a quote from a source who was present at the time. You may use a quote from the book *Farewell to Manzanar* or from another related book. Be sure to give the name of the person who said the quote. Each time you introduce a new topic, start a new paragraph. The paragraphs in newspaper articles are usually about 6-10 sentences long, so keep that in consideration as well.

Include a byline that gives your name and a dateline that tells when and where the article was written.

Since this is a news article, it is not appropriate to include your personal opinion or to use words that describe anyone in an unfavorable way. As a reporter, you must report only the facts.

PEER EDITING

When you finish the rough draft of your newspaper article, ask another student to read it. After reading your rough draft, the student should tell you what he/she liked best about the work, which parts were difficult to understand, and ways in which your work could be improved. Reread your text considering your critic's comments, and make the revisions you think are necessary.

PROOFREADING

Do a final proofreading of your newspaper article, double-checking your grammar, spelling, organization, and the clarity of your ideas. Turn the article in to your teacher for grading. Follow your teacher's guidelines for completing the final draft of your paper.

WRITING EVALUATION FORM *Farewell to Manzanar*

Name _____ Date _____ Class _____

Writing Assignment # _____

Circle One For Each Item:

Composition	excellent	good	fair	poor
Style	excellent	good	fair	poor
Grammar	excellent	good	fair	poor (errors noted)
Spelling	excellent	good	fair	poor (errors noted)
Punctuation	excellent	good	fair	poor (errors noted)
Legibility	excellent	good	fair	poor (errors noted)

Strengths:

Weaknesses:

Comments/Suggestions:

Daily Lesson Plans *Farewell to Manzanar*

LESSON SIX

Objectives
1. To complete the prereading work for Part I: Chapters 7-11
2 To read Part I: Chapters 7-11
3. To review the main ideas and events in Part I: Chapters 7-11

Activity #1
Give students about fifteen minutes to do the prereading and vocabulary work for Chapters 7-11.

Activity #3
Give students most of the remainder of the period to silently read Chapters 7-11.

Activity #4
Allow about fifteen minutes at the end of the class period to go over the study questions together, Tell students they will have a quiz on Part I: Chapters 1-11 during the next class period. Give students time to go through their study guides and notes to see if they are missing any information. Provide assistance as necessary.

Daily Lesson Plans *Farewell to Manzanar*

LESSON SEVEN

Objectives
1. To check to see that students have done the require reading
2. To identify examples of figurative language in the book

Activity #1

Quiz--Distribute quizzes (multiple choice study questions for Part I: Chapters 1-11 and give students about twenty minutes to complete them. Correct and grade the papers as a class. You may want to have students exchange papers, or allow them to correct their own work. As an extra credit assignment, have students find the correct answers to any questions they missed, and rewrite any "false" answers to be true. Collect the quizzes for recording the grades.

Activity #2

Explain to students that a simile is a comparison that uses the words *like* or *as* to compare two unlike things. Write the following sentence from Part I Chapter 2 on the board as an example: "*The secondhand dealers had been prowling around for weeks, like wolves, offering humiliating prices for goods and furniture they knew many of us would have to sell sooner or later.*" Ask a volunteer to underline the simile (like wolves) and discuss how the simile paints a vivid picture for the reader.

Then explain that a metaphor compares two things without using the words like or as. Write the following sentence from Part I Chapter 11 on the board as an example: "*Half the sky was dark with a tide of sand pouring toward us.*" Explain that by using the words "a tide of sand" the author is comparing the sandstorm to an ocean tide.

Have students make two columns on a piece of paper and write the words Simile and Metaphor at the tops of the columns. Tell them to keep track of the smilies and metaphors as they read. As an extension, they can create their own similes and metaphors for events or people in the book.

Daily Lesson Plans *Farewell to Manzanar*

LESSON EIGHT

Objectives
1. To participate in a writing conference with the teacher
2. To revise Writing Assignment #1 based on the teacher's suggestions
3. To complete the prereading work for Part II: Chapters 12-15
4. To read Part II: Chapters 12-15

Activity #1
Call students individually to your desk or some other private area of the classroom. Discuss their papers from Writing Assignment #1. Use the completed Writing Evaluation form as a basis for your critique.

Activity #2
Students should use this class time (when they are not in conference with you) to do any of the following: work on their nonfiction reading assignment; revise Writing Assignment #1; complete the prereading work for Part II: Chapters 12-15; read those chapters; or to review the study guide questions and prereading vocabulary worksheets they have completed so far.

Daily Lesson Plans *Farewell to Manzanar*

LESSON NINE

Objectives:
1. To review the main ideas and events from Part II: Chapters 12-15
2. To become acquainted with Writing Assignment #2

Activity #1

Have students sit in small groups to answer the study questions. Tell each group to choose a spokesperson. Discuss the answers to the study guide questions with the class, having each spokesperson respond for their group.

Activity #2

Distribute Writing Assignment #2. Discuss the directions in detail and give students ample time to complete the assignment.

LESSON TEN

Objectives
1. To preview the study questions and vocabulary for Part II: Chapters 16-19
2. To read Part II: Chapters 16-19
3. To review the main ideas and events from Part II: Chapters 16-19

Activity #1

Divide the class into small groups. Have the groups work together to do the prereading and vocabulary work. Group members can decide how they want to approach the work. Suggest that they may want to assign a few vocabulary words to each member, and have each member teach those vocabulary words to the rest of the group. Or, they may have each member work independently, then gather as a group to go over the vocabulary words.

Activity #2

Tell students to stay in the same groups as they formed to complete Activity #1. Have them sit in a small circle and take turns reading aloud quietly. As they come to the answer to one of the study questions, they should stop, discuss the question and answer, and write their response.

Activity #3

Have students sit with the groups they formed for the first two activities to answer the study questions. Tell each group to choose a spokesperson. Discuss the answers to the study guide questions with the class, having each spokesperson respond for their group.

WRITING ASSIGNMENT #2 *Farewell to Manzanar*
Writing to Persuade

PROMPT
In Part II Chapter 16 Jeanne briefly describes three of the court cases filed by Japanese-Americans against the internment. Read this section of Chapter 16 before you begin working on this writing assignment.

Then take the point of view of a non-Japanese American citizen who is reading about the internment. You have formed a group to protest the internment. Write to the government on behalf of your group to try and persuade the officials to release the Japanese-Americans.

PREWRITING
Make a list of the reasons you and your group think the Japanese-Americans should be released. Think of statements to support each of your reasons, and list them under each reason. Then number the reasons in order from most to least important.

DRAFTING
Make an introductory statement in which you describe the problem and the supposed reasons for the internment. Then briefly outline how the internment had affected the Japanese-Americans. Next, state your request.

Then use one paragraph for each of the reasons you think the people should be released. Use the supporting statements for each reason.

Summarize your request and respectfully ask for a reply from the government by a certain date, possibly a week after receiving the letter.

PEER CONFERENCING/REVISING
When you finish the rough draft, ask another student to look at it. You may want to give the student your checklist so he/she can double check for you and see that you have included all of the information. After reading, he or she should tell you what he/she liked best about your persuasive letter, which parts were difficult to understand or needed more information, and ways in which your work could be improved. Reread your persuasive letter considering your critic's comments and make the corrections you think are necessary.

PROOFREADING/EDITING
Do a final proofreading of your persuasive letter, double-checking your grammar, spelling, organization, and the clarity of your ideas.

FINAL DRAFT
Follow your teacher's guidelines for completing the final draft of your paper.

Daily Lesson Plans *Farewell to Manzanar*

LESSON ELEVEN

Objectives
1. To distinguish between fact and opinion in the book
2. To complete the prereading work for Part II: Chapters 20-21
3. To read Part II: Chapters 20-21

Activity #1
Write the following two sentences on the board:
> *That car is red.*
> *That car is awesome.*

Explain to students that the first sentence gives a fact about the car; the color of the car is red. A fact is a statement that can be proved. The color of the car can be proved to be red. The second sentence gives an opinion about the car. The opinion cannot definitely be proved. One person might think the car is awesome, but someone else might disagree.

Tell students that in the book, Jeanne gives facts as well as opinions. For example, in Chapter 3 she says, "*Woody stood up very straight, which in itself was funny, since he was only about five-foot-six.*" *Standing straight* and *five-foot-six* are facts, while *funny* is an opinion. Write the words *Facts* and *Opinions* at the tops of two pieces of chart paper. Tell half the class to look through the book for facts and the other half to look for opinions, and to write their findings on the correct chart. Give students about ten or fifteen minutes to work. Then read the facts and opinions aloud. Discuss how the facts can be proved. Tell students to continue being aware of facts and opinions as they finish reading the book.

Activity #2
Allow students to work individually or with partners to complete the prereading vocabulary work and to review the study guide questions.

Activity #3
Allow students to work individually or with partners to read the chapters. They can start answering the study guide questions if they have time. Remind them that the reading and study guide questions must be completed by the next class meeting.

Daily Lesson Plans *Farewell to Manzanar*

LESSON TWELVE

Objectives
1. To review the main ideas and events in Part II: Chapters 20-21
2. To complete the prereading work for Part III: Chapter 22
3. To read Part III: Chapter 22

Activity #1
Have each student write the letters A, B, C and D on separate index cards. Make an overhead transparency copy of the multiple choice questions for Part II: Chapters 20-21. Read the questions and answer choices aloud and have students hold up the letter that shows their answer choice. Discuss the answers with students. Have them find the answers in the book if they are unsure of an answer.

Activity #2
Give students about ten minutes to complete the prereading vocabulary worksheets and to go over the study guide questions.

Activity #3
Give students the rest of the class period to read the chapters and answer the study guide questions.

Daily Lesson Plans *Farewell to Manzanar*

LESSON THIRTEEN

Objectives
    1. To discuss the main ideas and events in Part III: Chapter 22
    2. To discuss *Farewell to Manzanar* at the interpretive and critical levels

Activity #1
    Ask volunteers to read their answers to the questions. Remind students to make corrections on their papers.

Activity #2
    Choose the questions from the Extra Writing Assignments/Discussion Questions which seem most appropriate for your students. A class discussion of these questions is most effective if students have been given the opportunity to formulate answers to the questions prior to the discussion. To this end, you may either have all the students formulate answers to all the questions, divide the class into groups, and assign one or more questions to each group, or you could assign one question to each student in your class. The option you choose will make a difference in the amount of class time needed for this activity.

Activity #3
    After students have had ample time to formulate answers to the questions, begin your class discussion of the questions and the ideas presented by the questions. Be sure students take notes during the discussion so they have information to study for the unit test.

Daily Lesson Plans *Farewell to Manzanar*

LESSON FOURTEEN

Student Objective
    1. To write a personal opinion paper

Activity #1
    Write the word *opinion* on the board and ask students what it means. Invite them to give their opinions on topics such as what should be served for lunch in the school cafeteria, if the school should have a dress code, their favorite singer/group. Ask other students to agree or disagree, and state their reasons. Make the point that all people have opinions. A person expressing an opinion should be able to back it up with facts and reasons why he/she has the opinion.

Activity #2
    Distribute copies of Writing Assignment #3. Go over the assignment in detail with the students. Tell them they will have the remainder of the class period to begin working on the assignment. Give the due date for the completed assignment. It should be a few days before the test.

EXTRA WRITING ASSIGNMENT/DISCUSSION QUESTIONS
Farewell to Manzanar

Interpretive
1. From what point of view is the novel written? How does this affect your understanding of the story?
2. Discuss the theme of overcoming prejudice as it is presented in the novel.
3. Discuss Jeanne's emergence as a person, and the roles that Mama, Papa, and her friends and teachers had in her development.
4. What are the main conflicts in the story? How are they resolved?
5. How important is the setting to the story?
6. Discuss the use of the pear tree as a symbol in the novel.
7. In the book, Jeanne compares her father to a slave set free after the Civil War. How do you respond to this comparison? Do you agree or disagree? Why?
8. Why did Papa burn his flag and papers?
9. Jeanne says that her life really started at Manzanar. What does she mean?
10. In Chapter 13, Jeanne describes the way Reiko and Mitsue treated her. Why do you think they did this?

Critical
11. How does the title fit with the themes in the book?
12. How did Jeanne change over the course of the book? Were the changes for the good?
13. How did Papa change over the course of the book? Were the changes for the good?
14. What was the overall mood of the book? Give examples to support your answer.
15. Discuss the imagery used in the book. How vivid is it? How effective is it?
16. During the course of the book, Jeanne strays from the straight sequence and gives some of the background on her parents. How does this organization affect your understanding and enjoyment of the book?
17. The book ends with a flashback to the day the family left Manzanar. How effective is this ending? How else might the authors have ended the book?
18. Jeanne mentions several other family members but does not go into detail about them. Does this lack of description add to or take away from the book?

Personal Response
19. Did you enjoy reading *Farewell to Manzanar*? Why or why not?
20. *Farewell to Manzanar* had several tragic or difficult circumstances. Which was the hardest, and why?
21. Which of the characters did you like, and why? Which did you dislike, and why?
22. This book is a memoir, written in first person. How do you think you would respond differently if the book were written in third person?
23. Which scene or event in the book did you like most? Why?
24. Which scene or event in the book was most upsetting or disturbing? Why?
25. Before you read the book, did you think it would be possible to live in an internment camp? What do you think after reading *Farewell to Manzanar*?
26. Did Jeanne's experiences change the way you look at yourself? How?

Extra Writing Assignment/discussion Questions, Continued

27. Does the author's presentation of the situation make it real for you?
28. Have you read any other stories similar to *Farewell to Manzanar?* If so, tell about them.
29. Would you recommend this book to another student? Why or why not?
30. If you could change one thing about the book, what would it be?
31. What questions would you like to ask the authors?

<u>Quotations</u>: Discuss the significance of the following quotations from the book.

1. Chizu said to Mama, "What does he mean? What is Pearl Harbor?"
    Mama yelled at him, "What is Pearl Harbor?"

2. "Woody, we can't live like this. Animals live like this."

3. "Probably hotcakes with soy sauce," Kiyo said, on his hands and knees between the bunks.
    "No." Woody grinned, heading out the door. "Rice. With Log Cabin Syrup and melted butter."

4. "He didn't die there, but things finished for him there, whereas for me it was like a birthplace. The camp was where our life lines intersected."

5. "Whatever he did had flourish."

6. "When your mother and father are having a fight, do you want them to kill each other? Or do you want them to stop fighting?"

7. "You be quiet. Listen to what I am saying. These idiots won't even get to the front gate of this camp. You watch. Before this is over, somebody is going to be killed. I guarantee it. They might all be killed."

8. "What the hell are you doing out here?" he yelled. "We're the reservoir crew."

9. "Do you want me to answer NO NO, Papa?"

10. At the meeting, when Papa stood up to defend the YES YES position, murmurs of *"Inu, inu"* began to circulate around the mess hall.

11. "We're here," Woody would say. "We're here, and there's no use moaning about it forever."

12. But this time, when she came to the door and called 'Wakatsuki-san?' he met her there shouting, "No! No baptism!"

13. "And now what will you do? Papa said. "I have to go." "What if you refused to answer the letter?" "It's my duty."

Extra Writing Assignment/discussion Questions, Continued

14. "Those images, of course, had come from my past. What I had to face now, a year later, was the future."

15. "See you in New Jersey. Find us all a big house back there."

16. "Your father was buried here in nineteen thirteen."

17. "One of the amazing things about America is the way it can both undermine you and keep you believing in your own possibilities, pumping you with hope."

18. "I wouldn't be faced with physical attack, or with overt shows of hatred. Rather, I would be seen someone foreign, or as someone other than American, or perhaps not be seen at all."

19. "If she doesn't make carnival queen this year," Leonard went on smugly, "she'll never be queen of anything anywhere for the rest of her life."

20. "Remembering now, I realized I had never forgotten his final outburst of defiance. But for the first time I saw it clearly, as clearly as the gathered desert stones, and when I left today for good I would carry that image with me again, as the rest of my inheritance."

WRITING ASSIGNMENT #3 *Farewell to Manzanar*
Personal Opinion

PROMPT

You are a junior high or high school classmate of Jeanne's. You see how she is treated by the other students. One of the students asks your opinion about how the Japanese-Americans should be treated. You share your opinion with the student.

PREWRITING

First, read through the book to find examples of the way Jeanne was treated. Ask yourself how you would feel if you were treated in a similar way. Then ask yourself what you would do if you had been in school with Jeanne. Make notes on paper to refer to later on as you write.

DRAFTING

Since this writing assignment is meant to be spoken, your writing style can be more informal than usual. Explain your position in the first few sentences. Back up your position with personal experiences or facts. Include ideas about how you feel and how you think the prejudicial words and actions make Jeanne and other Japanese-Americans feel.

PEER CONFERENCE/REVISING

When you finish the rough draft, ask another student to look at it. You may want to give the student your brainstorm list so he/she can double check for you and see that you have included all of the information. After reading, he or she should tell you what he/she liked best about your opinion paper, which parts were difficult to understand or needed more information, and ways in which your work could be improved. Reread your opinion paper considering your critic's comments and make the corrections you think are necessary.

PROOFREADING/EDITING

Do a final proofreading of your opinion paper, double-checking your grammar, spelling, organization, and the clarity of your ideas.

FINAL DRAFT

Follow your teacher's directions for making a final copy of your paper.

Daily Lesson Plans *Farewell to Manzanar*

LESSON FIFTEEN *Farewell to Manzanar*

Objectives
    1. To conduct library research for the Nonfiction Reading Assignment
    2. To complete any unfinished assignments

Activity #1
    Take the students to the library/media center for the entire class period. Tell them they can have the time to work on their Nonfiction Reading Assignment. Provide guidance in using the catalog and in finding resources as necessary. Students who have completed the assignment can complete other unfinished assignments related to the novel unit, or they can use the time to read for pleasure.

Daily Lesson Plans *Farewell to Manzanar*

LESSON SIXTEEN

Objective
> To review all of the vocabulary work done in this unit

VOCABULARY REVIEW ACTIVITIES

1. Divide your class into two teams and have an old-fashioned spelling or definition bee.

2. Give individuals or groups of students a *Farewell to Manzanar* Vocabulary Word Search Puzzle with a word list. The person (group) to find all of the vocabulary words in the puzzle first wins.

3. Give students a *Farewell to Manzanar* Vocabulary Word Search Puzzle without the word list. The person or group to find the most vocabulary words in the puzzle wins.

4. Put a *Farewell to Manzanar* Vocabulary Crossword Puzzle onto a transparency on the overhead projector and do the puzzle together as a class.

5. Give students a *Farewell to Manzanar* Vocabulary Matching Worksheet to do.

6. Use words from the word jumble page and have students spell them correctly, then use them in original sentences.

7. Play Vocabulary Bingo with the materials enclosed with this unit. The Caller calls out definitions for the vocabulary words. If a student has that word on his/her card, that word is covered with a piece of paper. When someone gets a column, row, or diagonal filled-in he/she yells out, "Bingo!" and wins that round.

8. Have students write a story in which they correctly use as many vocabulary words as possible. Have students read their compositions orally. Post the most original compositions on your bulletin board.

9. Have students work in teams and play charades with the vocabulary words.

10. Select a word of the day and encourage students to use it correctly in their writing and speaking vocabulary.

11. Have a contest to see which students can find the most vocabulary words used in other sources. You may want to have a bulletin board available so the students can write down their word, the sentence it was used in, and the source.

12. Assign a word to each student, or let them choose a word. Have them look up the origin of the word, the part of speech, definition, a synonym, and an antonym. Then have them write a sentence using the word. Have students present their information orally to the class.

Daily Lesson Plans *Farewell to Manzanar*

LESSON SEVENTEEN

Objective
	To review the main ideas presented in *Farewell to Manzanar*

Activity #1
	Choose one of the review games/activities included in the packet and spend your class period as outlined there.

Activity #2
	Remind students of the date for the Unit Test. Stress the review of the Study Guides and their class notes as a last minute, brush-up review for homework.

REVIEW GAMES / ACTIVITIES

1. Ask the class to make up a unit test for *Farewell to Manzanar*. The test should have 4 sections: multiple choice, true/false, short answer and essay. Students may use 1/2 period to make the test, including a separate answer sheet, and then swap papers and use the other 1/2 class period to take a test a classmate has devised. (open book)

2. Take 1/2 period for students to make up true and false questions (including the answers). Collect the papers and divide the class into two teams. Draw a big tic-tac-toe board on the chalkboard. Make one team X and one team O. Ask questions to each side, giving each student one turn. If the question is answered correctly, that student's team's letter (X or O) is placed in the box. If the answer is incorrect, no mark is placed in the box. The object is to get three marks in a row like tic-tac-toe. You may want to keep track of the number of games won for each team.

3. Take 1/2 period for students to make up questions (true/false and short answer). Collect the questions. Divide the class into two teams. You'll alternate asking questions to individual members of teams A & B (like in a spelling bee). The question keeps going from A to B until it is correctly answered, then a new question is asked. A correct answer does not allow the team to get another question. Correct answers are +2 points; incorrect answers are -1 point.

4. Allow students time to quiz each other (in pairs) from their study guides and class notes.

5. Give students a *Farewell to Manzanar* crossword puzzle to complete.

6. Play *Farewell to Manzanar* bingo using the materials included with this unit. The Caller gives clues to which the students must know the one-word answer. If that answer appears on their cards, they place a piece of paper over that word. The first student to have a filled-in row, column, or diagonal (like bingo) wins! (You should have students call off their filled-in words to make sure that all of their responses were correct).

Daily Lesson Plans *Farewell to Manzanar*

LESSON SEVENTEEN, continued

7. Divide your class into two teams. Use the *Farewell to Manzanar* crossword words with their letters jumbled as a word list. Student 1 from Team A faces off against Student 1 from Team B. You write the first jumbled word on the board. The first student (1A or 1B) to unscramble the word wins the chance for his/her team to score points. If 1A wins the jumble, go to student 2A and give him/her a clue. He/she must give you the correct word which matches that clue. If he/she does, Team A scores a point, and you give student 3A a clue for which you expect another correct response. Continue giving Team A clues until some team member makes an incorrect response. An incorrect response sends the game back to the jumbled-word face off, this time with students 2A and 2B. Instead of repeating giving clues to the first few students of each team, continue with the student after the one who gave the last incorrect response on the team.

8. Take on the persona of "The Answer Person." Allow students to ask any question about the book. Answer the questions, or tell students where to look in the book to find the answer.

9. Students may enjoy playing charades with events from the story. Select a student to start. Give him/her a card with a scene or event from the story. Allow the players to use their books to find the scene being described. The first person to guess each charade performs the next one.

10. Play a categories-type quiz game. (A master is included in this Unit Plan). Make an overhead transparency of the categories form. Divide the class into teams of three or four players each. Have each team Choose a recorder and a banker. Choose a team to go first. That team will choose a category and point amount. Ask the question to the entire class.(Use the Study Guide Quiz and Vocabulary questions.) Give the teams one minute to discuss the answer and write it down. Walk around the room and check the answers. Each team that answers correctly receives the points. (Incorrect answers are not penalized; they just don't receive any points). Cross out that square on the playing board. Play continues until all squares have been used. The winning team is the one with the most points. You can assign bonus points to any square or squares you choose.

11. Have individual students draw scenes from the book. Display the scenes and have the rest of the class look in their books to find the chapter or section that is being depicted. The first student to find the correct scene then displays his or her picture. When the game is over, collect the pictures and put them in a binder for students to look at during their free time.

NOTE: If students do not need the extra review, omit this lesson and go on to the test.

QUIZ GAME *Farewell to Manzanar*

Part I: Foreword-Chronology, Terms	Part I: Chapters 1-6	Part I: Chapters 7-11	Part II: Chapters 12-21	Part III: Chapter 22
100	100	100	100	100
200	200	200	200	200
300	300	300	300	300
400	400	400	400	400
500	500	500	500	500

LESSON EIGHTEEN

Objective
　　To test the students' understanding of the main ideas and themes in *Farewell to Manzanar*

Activity #1
　　Distribute the *v Farewell to Manzanar* Unit Tests. Go over the instructions in detail and allow the students the entire class period to complete the exam.

Activity #2
　　Collect all test papers and assigned books prior to the end of the class period.

NOTES ABOUT THE UNIT TESTS IN THIS UNIT:

There are 5 different unit tests which follow.

There are two short answer tests which are based primarily on facts from the novel. The answer key for short answer unit test 1 follows the student test. The answer key for short answer test 2 follows the student short answer unit test 2.

There is one advanced short answer unit test. It is based on the extra discussion questions. Use the matching key for short answer unit test 2 to check the matching section of the advanced short answer unit test. There is no key for the short answer questions. The answers will be based on the discussions you have had during class.

There are two multiple choice unit tests. Following the two unit tests, you will find an answer sheet on which students should mark their answers. The same answer sheet should be used for both tests; however, students' answers will be different for each test. Following the students' answer sheet for the multiple choice tests you will find your two keys: one for multiple choice test 1 and one for multiple choice test 2. If you follow the directions at the top of each of those pages, you should be able to overlay your answer key on the students' answer sheets and easily grade the papers.

The short answer tests have a vocabulary section. You should choose 10 of the vocabulary words from this unit, read them orally and have the students write them down. Then, either have students write a definition or use the words in sentences. The second part of the vocabulary test is matching.

Daily Lesson Plans *Farewell to Manzanar*

LESSON NINEEEN

Objectives
  1. To widen the breadth of students' knowledge about the topics discussed or touched upon in *Farewell to Manzanar*
  2. To present the nonfiction assignments

Activity #1
  Ask each student to give a brief oral report about the nonfiction work he/she read for the nonfiction assignment. Your criteria for evaluating this report will vary depending on the level of your students. You may wish for students to give the complete report without using notes of any kind. Or you may want students to read directly from a written report. You may want to do something between these two options. Make students aware of your criteria in ample time for them to prepare their reports.
  Start with one student's report. After that, ask if anyone else in the class has read on a topic related to the first student's report. If no one has, choose another student at random. After each report, be sure to ask if anyone has a report related to the one just completed. That will help keep continuity during the discussion of the reports.

Activity #2
  Collect the students' written reports. Put them in a binder and have the binder available for students to read.

Activity #3
If the class or school has a Web site, post the nonfiction reports there.

UNIT TESTS

SHORT ANSWER UNIT TEST 1 *Farewell to Manzanar*

I. Matching/Identification: Directions: Place the letter of the matching definition on the blank line.

_____ 1. Issei   A. Jeanne's home after released from internment

_____ 2. Nisei   B. beaten at camp and almost died

_____ 3. Sansei   C. Jeanne's friend in junior high but not high school

_____ 4. Ocean Park   D. evacuees begin to arrive at Manzanar

_____ 5. Cabrillo Homes   E. first generation, born in Japan

_____ 6. Radine   F. Jeanne's sister, had a baby at the camp

_____ 7. Fred Tayama   G. Jeanne's home before the internment

_____ 8. Eleanor   H. second generation, born in U. S. before WWII

_____ 9. March 25, 1942   I. Manzanar camp officially closes

_____ 10. Nov. 21, 1945   J. third generation, born in U. S. after WWII

II. Short Answer
Directions: Answer each question.

1. Describe the three events that occurred in 1942.

2. What was Order 9066 and how did it affect the Japanese Americans?

Short Answer Unit Test 1 *Farewell to Manzanar*

3. How does Jeanne describe the entire situation at the camp?

4. How does Jeanne as an adult see the cane that Papa brought back with him from Fort Lincoln?

5. Describe the riot. Include the causes, results, and the name of the leader.

6. How does Jeanne describe the results of the Loyalty Oath?

Short Answer Unit Test 1 *Farewell to Manzanar*

7. What does Jeanne say the camp became as the months turned into years? Explain what she meant by this.

8. Jeanne said she had a foretaste of being hated. How did she say she would have to respond? How did she feel about it?

9. What important event happened to Jeanne during her senior year in high school? What was Papa's response to the knowledge of this event? How did Jeanne respond?

10. How did the trip back to Manzanar as an adult help Jeanne?

Short Answer Unit Test 1 *Farewell to Manzanar*

III. Quotations: Identify the speaker and discuss the significance of each of the following quotations.

1. "What does he mean? What is Pearl Harbor?" / "What is Pearl Harbor?"

2. "When your mother and father are having a fight, do you want them to kill each other? Or do you want them to stop fighting?"

3. "Do you want me to answer NO NO, Papa?"

4. But this time, when she came to the door and called 'Wakatsuki-san?' he met her there shouting, "No! No baptism!"

5. "If she doesn't make carnival queen this year," _____ went on smugly, "she'll never be queen of anything anywhere for the rest of her life."

Short Answer Unit Test 1 *Farewell to Manzanar*

IV: Essay
    Jeanne says that her life really started at Manzanar. What does she mean?

Short Answer Unit Test 1 *Farewell to Manzanar*

V. Vocabulary Part 1

    Listen to the vocabulary word and spell it. After you have spelled all the words, go back and write down the definitions.

WORD	DEFINITION
1. _____	_____
2. _____	_____
3. _____	_____
4. _____	_____
5. _____	_____
6. _____	_____
7. _____	_____
8. _____	_____
9. _____	_____
10. _____	_____

Vocabulary Part 2: Place the letter of the matching definition on the blank line.

_____ 1. internment   A. violent

_____ 2. aliens   B. arousing public awareness and feeling

_____ 3. saboteur   C. ridiculous; absurd

_____ 4. turbulent   D. stubbornness

_____ 5. imperiously   E. being forced to stay in a place

_____ 6. grotesque   F. accepting what comes without complaint

_____ 7. credo   G. beliefs

_____ 8. resigned   H. person who harms an enemy nation

_____ 9. agitating   I. non-citizens living in a country

_____ 10. obstinance   J. in an arrogant, domineering way

ANSWER KEY SHORT ANSWER UNIT TEST 1 *Farewell to Manzanar*

I. Matching/Identification: Place the letter of the matching definition on the blank line.

E	1. Issei	A.	Jeanne's home after released from internment
H	2. Nisei	B.	beaten at camp and almost died
J	3. Sansei	C.	Jeanne's friend in junior high but not high school
G	4. Ocean Park	D.	evacuees begin to arrive at Manzanar
A	5. Cabrillo Homes	E.	first generation, born in Japan
C	6. Radine	F.	Jeanne's sister, had a baby at the camp
B	7. Fred Tayama	G.	Jeanne's home before the internment
F	8. Eleanor	H.	second generation, born in U. S. before WWII
D	9. March 25, 1942	I.	Manzanar camp officially closes
I	10. Nov. 21, 1945	J.	third generation, born in U. S. after WWII

II. Short Answer

1. Describe the three events that occurred in 1942.
   1. February 19. President Roosevelt gives the War Department the authority to define military areas in the western states and to exclude anyone who might be a threat.
   2. March 25. Evacuees begin to arrive at the Manzanar camp.
   3. August 12. Evacuation of 110,000 people of Japanese ancestry to ten inland camps is completed.

2. What was Order 9066 and how did it affect the Japanese Americans?
   Order 9066 authorized the War Department to define military areas in the western states and to exclude anyone who might be considered a threat to the war effort. The Japanese were talking about the possibility that they would be moved to some place inland.

3. How does Jeanne describe the entire situation at the camp?
   "All this was an open insult to the private self, a slap in the face you were powerless to challenge."

Answer Key Short Answer Unit Test 1 *Farewell to Manzanar*

4. How does Jeanne as an adult see the cane that Papa brought back with him from Fort Lincoln?
   She sees the cane as "a sad, homemade version of the samurai sword his grandfather carried in the land around Hiroshima."

5. Describe the riot. Include the causes, results, and the name of the leader.
   The day after Fred was beaten, three men were identified, and one was sent to the county jail. This man had been trying to organize a Kitchen Workers' Union in the camp. The beating and arrest caused a riot. The leader of the riot was Joe Kurihara. He demanded that the cook be brought back to the camp, and the authorities agreed. Later that same day, part of the mob went to the hospital to kill Fred Tayama. Some of the men went after others they thought were sympathizers. The part of the mob that went to the police station after the cook met up with the military police while they were still inside the camp. A fight started, and the MPs fired weapons and threw tear gas bombs. This action stopped the riot but two men died and ten were injured.

6. How does Jeanne describe the results of the Loyalty Oath?
   She said the results would have been comical if they had not been so grotesque. An espionage agent would not admit to being disloyal, while the Japanese who were loyal to America were so outraged at being made to take the oath that they turned anti-American.

7. What does Jeanne say the camp became as the months turned into years? Explain what she meant by this.
   The camp became its own world. People seemed to forget the war and only think of the next task that had to be done. They tried to create normalcy and keep any anger under control.

8. Jeanne said she had a foretaste of being hated. How did she say she would have to respond? How did she feel about it?
   She said she would allow someone to look at her with hatred because she thought she must have deserved it. She felt humiliated that someone could hate her and her family. She wanted to stay inside the camp and not face the prejudice.

9. What important event happened to Jeanne during her senior year in high school? What was Papa's response to the knowledge of this event? How did Jeanne respond?
   She was elected the school carnival queen. Papa enrolled Jeanne in a traditional Japanese odori class to learn Japanese ways. Jeanne lasted for ten lessons before the teacher sent her away.

Answer Key Short Answer Unit Test 1 *Farewell to Manzanar*

10. How did the trip back to Manzanar as an adult help Jeanne?
    It helped her realize that her life really began at Manzanar. The trip helped her understand the bits of the place that she still carried within her.

III. Quotations: Identify the speaker and discuss the significance of each of the following quotations.

1. "What does he mean? What is Pearl Harbor?" / "What is Pearl Harbor?"
    In Chapter 1, the fishing boats turn back to shore unexpectedly. The women hear a man on the wharf yelling that the Japanese have bombed Pearl Harbor. Chizu, who is Woody's wife, asks the first question. Mama responds with a question of her own.

2. "When your mother and father are having a fight, do you want them to kill each other? Or do you want them to stop fighting?"
    Papa is being interviewed at Fort Lincoln. The interviewer asks him who he wants to win the war.

3. "Do you want me to answer NO NO . . . ?"
    Woody and Papa are discussing the Loyalty Oath. Papa wants to know how Woody will answer the questions. He is not pleased to learn that Woody will fight in the U. S. army. Woody asks Papa if he should answer NO NO to the questions on the oath. Papa responds that Woody cannot do that, or he will be sent back to Japan.

4. But this time, when she came to the door and called 'Wakatsuki-san?' he met her there shouting, "No! No baptism!"
    Jeanne has announced her intentions to get baptized and confirmed Catholic. A Maryknoll nun named Sister Bernadette came to the house to visit Papa and he tells her that Jeanne is not allowed to convert.

5. "If she doesn't make carnival queen this year," ____ went on smugly, "she'll never be queen of anything anywhere for the rest of her life."
    Jeanne has been nominated for high school carnival queen. She finds out from her friend Leonard that some of the teachers are trying to alter the vote so she won't win. Jeanne says she can't do anything about it, but Leonard says he will. He goes into the office and threatens to tell the entire student body about the deception unless it stops. Jeanne wins.

Answer Key Short Answer Unit Test 1 *Farewell to Manzanar*

V. Vocabulary Part 1 Write in the words you chose and their definitions if you choose.

WORD	DEFINITION
1.	
2.	
3.	
4.	
5.	
6.	
7.	
8.	
9.	
10.	

Vocabulary Part 2: Place the letter of the matching definition on the blank line.

E	1. internment	A.	violent
I	2. aliens	B.	arousing public awareness and feeling
H	3. saboteur	C.	ridiculous; absurd
A	4. turbulent	D.	stubbornness
J	5. imperiously	E.	being forced to stay in a place
C	6. grotesque	F.	accepting what comes without complaint
G	7. credo	G.	beliefs
F	8. resigned	H.	person who harms an enemy nation
B	9. agitating	I.	non-citizens living in a country
D	10. obstinance	J.	in an arrogant, domineering way

SHORT ANSWER UNIT TEST 2 *Farewell to Manzanar*

I. Matching/Identification: Place the letter of the matching definition on the blank line.

_____ 1. San Jose   A. led a dance band; sent to Germany

_____ 2. Woody Wakatsuki   B. location of the first barracks the family lived in

_____ 3. New Jersey   C. punched Papa in the face to protect Mama

_____ 4. Bill Wakatsuki   D. CA; location of Manzanar camp

_____ 5. Executive Order 9066 E. second barracks, larger quarters

_____ 6. Owens Valley   F. allowed Japanese-Americans to become U. S. citizens

_____ 7. Kiyo Wakatsuki   G. allowed the military to exclude people from Western areas

_____ 8. Public Law 414   H. CA; family home for Jeanne's last year in high school

_____ 9. Block 16   I. drafted into the U.S. Army, visited Japan

_____ 10. Block 28   J. several of Jeanne's family members moved here after war

II. Short Answer

1. What restriction did the U. S. Bureau of Immigration and Naturalization create for the Japanese, and when was this done?

2. Why was the FBI picking up Japanese-American fishermen?

Short Answer Unit Test 2 *Farewell to Manzanar*

3. Describe the conditions in the barracks.

4. What happened in the mess halls that changed the families? Why did this happen?

5. Why were the women calling papa "inu"?

6. What were the two questions on the Loyalty Oath? How did Papa answer the questions on the Loyalty Oath? Why did he answer that way?

Short Answer Unit Test 2 *Farewell to Manzanar*

7. What did the residents do to make the camp livable?

8. Describe the three Supreme Court cases involving the camps.

9. 9. Jeanne says the family left the camp "in style." Describe this. Explain why Papa did this.

10. How did Jeanne view her situation when it was happening and also as an adult looking back when she wrote the book?

Short Answer Unit Test 2 *Farewell to Manzanar*

III. Quotations: Identify the speaker and discuss the significance of each of the following quotations.

1. "You be quiet. Listen to what I am saying. These idiots won't even get to the front gate of this camp. You watch. Before this is over, somebody is going to be killed. I guarantee it. They might all be killed."

2. "Probably hotcakes with soy sauce," ____ said, on his hands and knees between the bunks. "No." ____ grinned, heading out the door. "Rice. With Log Cabin Syrup and melted butter."

3. "Your father was buried here in nineteen thirteen."

4. "____, we can't live like this. Animals live like this."

5. "I wouldn't be faced with physical attack, or with overt shows of hatred. Rather, I would be seen as someone foreign, or as someone other than American, or perhaps not be seen at all."

Short Answer Unit Test 2 *Farewell to Manzanar*

IV: Essay

How did Papa change over the course of the book? Why did these changes occur? Were the changes for the good?

Short Answer Unit Test 2 *Farewell to Manzanar*

V: Vocabulary

Directions: Write down the vocabulary word your teacher says. Then go back and write down the correct definition for each word.

ANSWER KEY SHORT ANSWER UNIT TEST 2 *Farewell to Manzanar*

I. Matching/Identification

H	1. San Jose	A. led a dance band; sent to Germany
I	2. Woody Wakatsuki	B. location of the first barracks the family lived in
J	3. New Jersey	C. punched Papa in the face to protect Mama
A	4. Bill Wakatsuki	D. CA; location of Manzanar camp
G	5. Executive Order 9066	E. second barracks, larger quarters
D	6. Owens Valley	F. allowed Japanese-Americans to become U. S. citizens
C	7. Kiyo Wakatsuki	G. allowed the military to exclude people from Western areas
F	8. Public Law 414	H. CA; family home for Jeanne's last year in high school
B	9. Block 16	I. drafted into the U.S. Army, visited Japan
E	10. Block 28	J. several of Jeanne's family members moved here after war

II. Short Answer

1. What restriction did the U. S. Bureau of Immigration and Naturalization create for the Japanese, and when was this done?
    In 1911 the U. S. Bureau of Immigration and Naturalization said that only whites and people of African descent could file for citizenship. The Japanese were not allowed to file for U. S. citizenship.

2. Why was the FBI picking up Japanese-American fishermen?
    The FBI thought the Japanese-American fishermen might be contacting enemy Japanese ships off the western coast of the US, and possibly supplying them with oil

Answer Key Short Answer Unit Test 2 *Farewell to Manzanar*
Short Answer, continued

3. Describe the conditions in the barracks.

    The barracks had been divided into small units and were crowded. Dust and wind blew in from the outside through cracks in the walls. The only furniture was Army surplus cots, blankets, and mattress covers.

4. What happened in the mess halls that changed the families? Why did this happen?

    In the mess halls they stopped eating as a family. Granny was not able to walk to the mess hall, so Mama brought her food to the barracks. The children ate with their friends. Sometimes the children went to a different block if they heard the cook there was good. After three years of eating in the mess hall, Jeanne's family collapsed as an integrated unit.

5. Why were the women calling papa "inu"?

    The word *inu* means collaborator or informer. Anyone who cooperated with the camp authorities was considered *inu*. Papa had been released from Fort Lincoln earlier than some of the other men because the Justice Department could not find any reason to keep him. When he got to Manzanar, a rumor went around the camp that when he was interpreting for the military authorities at Fort Lincoln he got information from other Japanese prisoners and gave it to the authorities to buy his release. None of this was true.

6. What were the two questions on the Loyalty Oath? How did Papa answer the questions on the Loyalty Oath? Why did he answer that way?

    The one question asked if the signer was willing to serve in the United States Armed Forces on combat duty. The second question asked if the signer would swear unqualified allegiance to the United States of America, defend the country from attack, and forswore any allegiance to Japan. Papa answered YES YES to the questions. He did this because he thought he was too old to start over if he were sent back to Japan, and to keep the family together at Manzanar. If he had answered NO NO, he would have been sent to a camp for the disloyal and eventually might have been sent back to Japan

Answer Key Short Answer Unit Test 2 *Farewell to Manzanar*
Short Answer, continued

7. What did the residents do to make the camp livable?

    They made the best of a bad situation. They planted gardens of all kinds, started a farm outside the gate, and built a park. They had beauty parlors, scout troops, churches, police and fire departments, and many other things that would be in an American small town.

8. Describe the three Supreme Court cases involving the camps.

    The first case a Nisei student named Gordon Hirabayashi challenged the racial bias of the evacuation order, and the violation of his civil rights. He also stayed out after curfew. The court did not rule on the evacuation order but said that during wartime the army had the right to impose a curfew and place restrictions on a racial group.

    In the second case, a Nisei named Fred Korematsu challenged the racial bias of the evacuation. To avoid internment, he had had plastic surgery and changed his name. The court sided with the army and allowed the evacuations. The third case challenged the actual internment. In April 1942 a Nisei woman named Mitsue Endo protested the internment under the right of habeas corpus. That meant a person could not be unjustly held against their will. The court agreed that the government did not have the authority to imprison loyal citizens against their will. Because of the ruling, the army started closing the camps and told the internees they were allowed to return to their homes.

9. Jeanne says the family left the camp "in style." Describe this. Explain why Papa did this.

    Papa bought a Nash sedan so the family could drive away from the camp. Papa bought the car as his final act of defiance.

10. How did Jeanne view her situation when it was happening and also as an adult looking back when she wrote the book?

    When she was a child she accepted the limitations placed on her and saw the situation as her fault. She thought she was creating a problem for the others. As an adult looking back, she is infuriated that she accepted things so readily.

Answer Key Short Answer Unit Test 2 *Farewell to Manzanar*

III. Quotations
Identify the speaker and discuss the significance of each of the following quotations.

1. "You be quiet. Listen to what I am saying. These idiots won't even get to the front gate of this camp. You watch. Before this is over, somebody is going to be killed. I guarantee it. They might all be killed."
 Papa is talking to Mama about the riot. He disagrees with the people in the camp who want to go back to Japan. He doesn't think they should be protesting the way they are.

2. "Probably hotcakes with soy sauce," ____ said, on his hands and knees between the bunks. "No." ____ grinned, heading out the door. "Rice. With Log Cabin Syrup and melted butter."
 It is the first morning in the camp. Kiyo makes a comment about breakfast and Woody answers. Their comments are based on the inedible dinner they were served the first night, when the Caucasian cooks gave the Japanese Americans what they thought was traditional food.

3. "Your father was buried here in nineteen thirteen."
 Woody is in Japan in 1946 visiting his father's family. His Aunt Toyo shows him the grave where the family symbolically buried his father because no one had heard from him for nine years after he left. They thought he was dead.

4. "____, we can't live like this. Animals live like this."
 Mama is talking to Woody in the barracks. It is the first morning after their arrival. She is upset at the amount of dust that has blown in through the cracks in the wallboards, and at the general condition in which they find themselves.

5. "I wouldn't be faced with physical attack, or with overt shows of hatred. Rather, I would be seen s someone foreign, or as someone other than American, or perhaps not be seen at all."
 Jeanne describes the way she will be treated in school when she returns to a regular public school after the internment is over.

Answer Key Short Answer Unit Test 2 *Farewell to Manzanar*

<u>IV: Essay</u>

How did Papa change over the course of the book? Why did these changes occur? Were the changes for the good?

(for teacher notes)

Answer Key Short Answer Unit Test 2 *Farewell to Manzanar*

V: Vocabulary

Directions: Write down the vocabulary word your teacher says. Then go back and write down the correct definiton for each word.

(for teacher notes)

Advanced Short Answer Unit Test *Farewell to Manzanar*

I. Matching/Identification

Directions: Place the letter of the matching definition on the blank line.

_____ 1. San Jose   A. led a dance band; sent to Germany

_____ 2. Woody Wakatsuki   B. location of the first barracks the family lived in

_____ 3. New Jersey   C. punched Papa in the face to protect Mama

_____ 4. Bill Wakatsuki   D. CA; location of Manzanar camp

_____ 5. Executive Order 9066 E. second barracks, larger quarters

_____ 6. Owens Valley   F. allowed Japanese-Americans to become U. S. citizens

_____ 7. Kiyo Wakatsuki   G. allowed the military to exclude people from Western areas

_____ 8. Public Law 414   H. CA; family home for Jeanne's last year in high school

_____ 9. Block 16   I. drafted into the U.S. Army, visited Japan

_____ 10. Block 28   J. several of Jeanne's family members moved here after war

II. Short Answer

1. Explain the chronology of the Japanese immigration to the United States from 1869 through 1952.

2. What event caused the internment of the Japanese Americans? Where were they taken? How long were they there? When and why were they released?

Advanced Short Answer Unit Test *Farewell to Manzanar*
II. Short Answer, continued

3. Describe the conditions at the Manzanar camp. Include the changes the residents made during their time at the camp.

4. Discuss Jeanne's emergence as a person, and the roles that Mama, Papa, her family, her friends and teachers had in her development.

5. Which scene or event in the book was most upsetting or disturbing? Why?

Advanced Short Answer Unit Test *Farewell to Manzanar*
III. Quotations
Directions: Identify the speaker and discuss the significance of each quotation.

1. "He didn't die there, but things finished for him there, whereas for me it was like a birthplace. The camp was where our life lines intersected."

2. "When your mother and father are having a fight, do you want them to kill each other? Or do you want them to stop fighting?"

3. At the meeting, when Papa stood up to defend the YES YES position, murmurs of "*Inu, inu*" began to circulate around the mess hall.

4. "And now what will you do? Papa said. "I have to go." "What if you refused to answer the letter?" "It's my duty."

5. "Remembering now, I realized I had never forgotten his final outburst of defiance. But for the first time I saw it clearly, as clearly as the gathered desert stones, and when I left today for good I would carry that image with me again, as the rest of my inheritance."

Advanced Short Answer Unit Test *Farewell to Manzanar*
III. Quotations, continued

6. "If she doesn't make carnival queen this year," Leonard went on smugly, "she'll never be queen of anything anywhere for the rest of her life."

7. "Your father was buried here in nineteen thirteen."

8. "See you in New Jersey. Find us all a big house back there."

9. "_____, we can't live like this. Animals live like this."

10. But this time, when she came to the door and called 'Wakatsuki-san?' he met her there shouting, "No! No baptism!"

Advanced Short Answer Unit Test *Farewell to Manzanar*
IV. Vocabulary

Directions: Listen to the words and write them down. After you have written down all of the words, write a paragraph in which you use all the words. The paragraph must in some way relate to the book *Farewell to Manzanar*.

Multiple Choice Unit Test 1 *Farewell to Manzanar*

I. Matching/Identification

_____ 1. Issei   A. Jeanne's home after released from internment

_____ 2. Nisei   B. beaten at camp and almost died

_____ 3. Sansei   C. Jeanne's friend in junior high but not high school

_____ 4. Ocean Park   D. evacuees begin to arrive at Manzanar

_____ 5. Cabrillo Homes   E. first generation, born in Japan

_____ 6. Radine   F. Jeanne's sister, had a baby at the camp

_____ 7. Fred Tayama   G. Jeanne's home before the internment

_____ 8. Eleanor   H. second generation, born in U. S. before WWII

_____ 9. March 25, 1942   I. Manzanar camp officially closes

_____ 10. Nov. 21, 1945   J. third generation, born in U. S. after WWII

II. Multiple Choice

1. What is the author's (Jeanne Wakatsuki Houston) relationship to Manzanar?
    A. She was a reporter doing a story about the camp.
    B. Her parents were interred there before she was born.
    C. Her husband's family was interred there when he was a boy.
    D. She was interred there with her family when she was a young girl.

2. True or False: In 1911 the U. S. Bureau of Immigration and Naturalization allowed the Japanese to file for U. S. citizenship.
    A. True
    B. False

3. The FBI thought the Japanese fishermen might be ___.
    A. poisoning the fish they caught
    B. contacting Japanese ships off the west coast
    C. trying to leave the U. S. and sail back to Japan
    D. smuggling enemy soldiers into the United States

Multiple Choice Unit Test 1 *Farewell to Manzanar*
II. Multiple Choice, continued

4. Which of the following does **not** describe the barracks?
    A. cracks in walls
    B. crowded
    C. dusty
    D. warm

5. For Mama, using the ____ was a humiliation that she never got used to.
    A. latrines
    B. public well
    C. English language
    D. second-hand clothing

6. According to Jeanne, which area of the camp caused her family to collapse as an integrated unit?
    A. school
    B. mess hall
    C. barracks
    D. Catholic church

7. As an adult, Jeanne compared her father's cane to ___.
    A. a crutch
    B. a baseball bat
    C. a samurai sword
    D. a diamond necklace

8. The second question on the Loyalty Oath asked the signers to do three things. Which of the following was **not** one of those things?
    A. forswear any allegiance to Japan
    B. defend the United States from attack
    C. swear unqualified allegiance to the United States
    D. change their first and last names to ones that sounded more "American"

9. What would Jeanne have done if she had been told she was free?
    A. run into the mountains
    B. go back to Long Beach
    C. move to the East Coast
    D. go right back to the camp

10. Jeanne said the family left the camp "in style." How did they do this?
    A. They all wore new clothes.
    B. They organized a parade to march out of the camp.
    C. They decorated the bus with streamers and flowers.
    D. Papa bought a Nash sedan and the family drove away.

Multiple Choice Unit Test 1 *Farewell to Manzanar*

III. Quotations
Direction: Match the two parts of each quotation.
1. "What does he mean?

2. "When your mother and father are having a fight, do you want them to kill each other?

3. "Do you want me to answer

4. But this time, when she came to the door and called 'Wakatsuki-san?'

5. "If she doesn't make carnival queen this year," Leonard went on smugly,

6. "These idiots won't even get to the front gate of this camp.

7. "Probably hotcakes with soy sauce," Kiyo said, on his hands and knees between the bunks.

8. "Your father

9. "Woody, we can't live like this.

10. "Rather, I would be seen as someone foreign,

A. he met her there shouting, "No! No baptism!"

B. Animals live like this."

C. What is Pearl Harbor?"

D. or as someone other than American, or perhaps not be seen at all."

E. NO NO, Papa?"

F. You watch. Before this is over, somebody is going to be killed."

G. "No." Woody grinned, heading out the door. "Rice. With Log Cabin Syrup and melted butter."

H. Or do you want them to stop fighting?"

I. was buried here in nineteen thirteen."

J. "she'll never be queen of anything anywhere for the rest of her life."

Multiple Choice Unit Test 1 *Farewell to Manzanar*

IV. Vocabulary Part 1
Directions: Match the word and its meaning.
1. careening   A. rules proclaimed by one in authority
2. idealist   B. happening after death
3. affirmed   C. violent
4. internment   D. being forced to stay in a place
5. edicts   E. watching
6. posthumous   F. keeping away
7. turbulent   G. declared to be true
8. vigil   H. rushing headlong with a swaying motion
9. warding   I. involuntary muscle contraction
10. spasm   J. person who wants things to be perfect

Vocabulary Part 2 Directions: Mark the letter next to the word that matches the definition.

11. dare to go
    a. oblivion
    b. venture
    c. intangible
    d. asunder

12. crouch in fear
    a. flourish
    b. livid
    c. cringe
    d. impact

13. squat; sit back on ones heels
    a. dwindle
    b. hunker
    c. resigned
    d. surplus

14. canceled
    a. rescinded.
    b. validation
    c. overt
    d. subdued

15. decision or choice
    a. stance
    b. priority
    c. filial
    d. volition

16. person who harms an enemy nation
    a. collaborator
    b. dredge
    c. Issei
    d. saboteur

17. out of place
    a. guileless
    b. incongruous
    c. chaos
    d. acquiescence

18. change of form or structure
    a. metamorphosis
    b. benevolent
    c. volition
    d. tinge

19. nourishment or support
    a. naturalization
    b. reservoir
    c. authentic
    d. sustenance

20. calm; serious
    a. congestion
    b. sedate
    c. asunder
    d. agitating

Multiple Choice Unit Test 2 *Farewell to Manzanar*

I. Matching/Identification

_____ 1. San Jose   A. led a dance band; sent to Germany

_____ 2. Woody Wakatsuki   B. location of the first barracks the family lived in

_____ 3. New Jersey   C. punched Papa in the face to protect Mama

_____ 4. Bill Wakatsuki   D. CA; location of Manzanar camp

_____ 5. Executive Order 9066   E. second barracks, larger quarters

_____ 6. Owens Valley   F. allowed Japanese-Americans to become U. S. citizens

_____ 7. Kiyo Wakatsuki   G. allowed the military to exclude people from Western areas

_____ 8. Public Law 414   H. CA; family home for Jeanne's last year in high school

_____ 9. Block 16   I. drafted into the U.S. Army, visited Japan

_____ 10. Block 28   J. several of Jeanne's family members moved here after war

II. Multiple Choice

1. In 1870 Congress granted naturalization rights to ____.
    A. Orientals only
    B. free whites, Orientals, and Mexicans
    C. free whites and people of African descent, but not Orientals
    D. people of African descent and people from the Middle East

2. What was the Supreme Court ruling of December 18, 1944?
    A. Anyone can be held in detention during wartime.
    B. All Japanese-Americans had to leave the country.
    C. The camps would remain open for six more years.
    D. Loyal citizens cannot be held in detention camps.

3. True or False: The night Papa heard the news about Pearl harbor, he celebrated by singing the Japanese national anthem.
    A. True
    B. False

Multiple Choice Unit Test 2 *Farewell to Manzanar*

II. Multiple Choice, continued

4. What job did Papa have at Fort Lincoln?
    A. auto mechanic
    B. radio operator
    C. prison guard
    D. interviewer

5. What happened to the Wakatsuki family?
    A. They were sent back to their own home.
    B. They were relocated to the Manzanar camp.
    C. They were allowed to stay in Boyle Heights.
    D. They were sent to stay with an American family in New Jersey

6. Jeanne described the situation as ____.
    A. a kick in the stomach
    B. a knife in the back
    C. a slap in the face
    D. a broken heart

7. How old is Jeanne in the first part of the story?
    A. 15
    B. 10
    C. 7
    D. 2

8. How did Papa answer the two questions on the Loyalty Oath?
    A. YES NO
    B. NO NO
    C. NO YES
    D. YES YES

9. What happened to Woody?
    A. he was drafted into the U. S. Army
    B. he was sent to another camp
    C. he was sent back to Japan
    D. he got cancer

10. What comparison did Jeanne use to describe Papa at the end of the book?
    A. like a slave freed after the Civil War
    B. like a little boy in a room full of new toys
    C. like a young man with his whole life ahead of him
    D. like an old man who could not walk without a

Multiple Choice Unit Test 2 *Farewell to Manzanar*

III. Quotations
Directions: Match the two parts of each quotation.

1. "If she doesn't make carnival queen this year," Leonard went on smugly,

2. "What the hell are you doing out here?" he yelled.

3. "He didn't die there, but things finished for him there, whereas for me it was

4. "And now what will you do? Papa said. "I have to go."

5. "We're here,

6. At the meeting, when Papa stood up to defend the YES YES position,

7. "No." Woody grinned, heading out the door.

8. "Those images, of course, had come from my past.

9. "Remembering now, I realized
10. ". . . and when I left today for good

A. "We're the reservoir crew."

B. "What if you refused to answer the letter?" "It's my duty."

C. "Rice. With Log Cabin Syrup and melted butter."

D. What I had to face now, a year later, was the future."

E. I would carry that image with me again, as the rest of my inheritance."

F. and there's no use moaning about it forever."

G. I had never forgotten his final outburst of defiance."

H. "she'll never be queen of anything anywhere for the rest of her life."

I. like a birthplace. The camp was where our life lines intersected."

J. murmurs of "*Inu, inu*" began to circulate around the mess hall.

Multiple Choice Unit Test 2 Farewell to Manzanar

IV. Vocabulary Part 1

Directions: Match the word and its meaning.

1. aliens
2. gouging
3. acquiescence
4. bias
5. intangible
6. obstinance
7. stance
8. marooned
9. confiscators
10. grotesque

A. authorities who take and keep things
B. ridiculous; absurd
C. digging; tearing out
D. not able to be seen or touched
E. left in a helpless position
F. agreement without objections
G. non-citizens living in a country
H. preference based on prejudice
I. stubbornness
J. manner of standing

Vocabulary Part 2

Directions: Mark the letter next to the word that matches the definition.

11. going away in different directions
    a. dispersing
    b. rescinding
    c. tittering
    d. sprinting

12. warnings of what is to come
    a. desolation
    b. premonitions
    c. edicts
    d. congestion

13. care taken before hand
    a. credo
    b. issue
    c. reservoir
    d. precautions

14. person who harms an enemy nation
    a. administrator
    b. saboteur
    c. dealer
    d. relative

15. being open to attack or injury
    a. cocky
    b. recurring
    c. vulnerability
    d. livid

16. state of agitation or disturbance
    a. metamorphosis
    b. turmoil
    c. trough
    d. oblivion

17. surrender on certain conditions
    a. affirm
    b. dredge
    c. capitulate
    d. recommend

18. in pieces or separate parts
    a. asunder
    b. turbulent
    c. enormous
    d. tremendous

19. dare to go
    a. dwindle
    b. assimilate
    c. gather
    d. venture

20. admitted to citizenship
    a. naturalization
    b. interred
    c. terminated
    d. confiscated

ANSWER SHEET Multiple Choice Unit Test 1, 2 *Farewell to Manzanar*

I. Matching	III. Quotations	IV. Vocabulary
1. _____	1.	1.
2.	2.	2.
3.	3.	3.
4.	4.	4.
5.	5.	5.
6.	6.	6.
7.	7.	7.
8.	8.	8.
9.	9.	9.
10.	10.	10.
		11.
		12.
		13.
		14.
		15.
		16.
		17.
		18.
		19.
		20.

II. Multiple Choice

1. (A) (B) (C) (D)
2. (A) (B) (C) (D)
3. (A) (B) (C) (D)
4. (A) (B) (C) (D)
5. A) (B) (C) (D)
6. (A) (B) (C) (D)
7. (A) (B) (C) (D)
8. (A) (B) (C) (D)
9. (A) (B) (C) (D)
10. (A) (B) (C) (D)

ANSWER SHEET KEY Multiple Choice Unit Test 1 *Farewell to Manzanar*

I. Matching		III. Quotations		IV. Vocabulary	
1.	E	1.	C	1.	H
2.	H	2.	H	2.	J
3.	J	3.	E	3.	G
4.	G	4.	A	4.	D
5.	A	5.	J	5.	A
6.	C	6.	F	6.	B
7.	B	7.	G	7.	C
8.	F	8.	I	8.	E
9.	D	9.	B	9.	F
10.	I	10.	D	10.	I
				11.	<u>B</u>
				12.	C
				13.	B
				14.	A
				15.	D
				16.	D
				17.	B
				18.	A
				19.	D
				20.	B

II. Multiple Choice

1. (A) (B) (C) ( )
2. (A) ( ) (C) (D)
3. (A) ( ) (C) (D)
4. (A) (B) (C) ( )
5. ( ) (B) (C) (D)
6. (A) ( ) (C) (D)
7. (A) (B) ( ) (D)
8. (A) (B) (C) ( )
9. (A) (B) (C) ( )
10. (A) (B) (C) ( )

ANSWER SHEET KEY Multiple Choice Unit Test 2 *Farewell to Manzanar*

I. Matching		III. Quotations		IV. Vocabulary	
1.	H	1.	H	1.	G
2.	I	2.	A	2.	C
3.	J	3.	I	3.	F
4.	A	4.	B	4.	H
5.	G	5.	F	5.	D
6.	D	6.	J	6.	I
7.	C	7.	C	7.	J
8.	F	8.	D	8.	E
9.	B	9.	G	9.	A
10.	E	10.	E	10.	B
				11.	<u>A</u>

II. Multiple Choice

1. (A) (B) ( ) (D)
2. (A) (B) (C) ( )
3. (A) ( ) (C) (D)
4. (A) (B) (C) ( )
5. A) ( ) (C) (D)
6. (A) (B) ( ) (D)
7. (A) (B) ( ) (D)
8. (A) (B) (C) ( )
9. ( ) (B) (C) (D)
10. ( ) (B) (C) (D)

12. B
13. D
14. B
15. C
16. B
17. C
18. A
19. D
20. A

UNIT RESOURCES

BULLETIN BOARD IDEAS *Farewell to Manzanar*

1. Save one corner of the board for the best of students' *Farewell to Manzanar* writing assignments. You may want to use background maps of California to represent the setting of the novel.

2. Take one of the word search puzzles from the extra activities packet and with a marker copy it over in a large size on the bulletin board. Write the clue words to find to one side. Invite students prior to and after class to find the words and circle them on the bulletin board.

3. Have students find or draw pictures that they think resemble the people and scenery in the book.

4. Invite students to help make an interactive bulletin board quiz. Give each student a half-sheet of paper (about 4"x5') folded in half so that it can open. On the outside flap, have each student write a description of one of the characters in the text. On the inside, they will write the name of the character. You can staple or tack these papers to the bulletin board so that the students can read the descriptions and lift the flaps to find the answers.

5. Collect and display pictures of Japan, Japanese-Americans, California during World War II, the resettlement camps, and the bombing of Pearl Harbor.

6. Display articles about people who were interred in the resettlement camps, and the actions the United States government has taken since the end of World War II to make restitution to the people.

7. Display articles about Jeanne Wakatsuki Houston.

8. Have students design postcards depicting the settings of the book.

9. Display a large map that includes the United States, the Pacific Ocean, and Japan. Have students locate the areas mentioned in the novel.

10. Display news clippings about World War II, especially those about the resettlement camps, Japanese-Americans, and the fight with the Japanese.

EXTRA ACTIVITIES PACKET *Farewell to Manzanar*

One of the difficulties in teaching a novel is that all students don't read at the same speed. One student who likes to read may take the book home and finish it in a day or two. Sometimes a few students finish the in-class assignments early. The problem, then, is finding suitable extra activities for students.

One thing that helps is to keep a little library in the classroom. For this unit on *Farewell to Manzanar* you might check out from the school or public library other books about World War II, the resettlement camps, and the Japanese immigrants who came to America.

Your students who have reading difficulties, or speak English as a second language may benefit from listening to all or part of the book on tape. *Farewell to Manzanar* is available commercially, or you may want to have an adult or a student who reads well tape record the book for you.

Other things you may keep on hand are word search puzzles. Several puzzles relating directly to *Farewell to Manzanar* are included in the unit. Feel free to duplicate them.

Some students may like to draw. You might devise a contest or allow some extra-credit grade for students who draw characters or scenes from *Farewell to Manzanar*. Note, too, that if the students do not want to keep their drawings you may pick up some extra bulletin board materials this way. If you have a contest and you supply the prize. You could, possibly, make the drawing itself a non-refundable entry fee.

Have maps, a globe, and travel brochures on hand for easy reference. Travel agencies and automobile clubs are good sources for these materials.

The pages which follow contain games, puzzles, and worksheets. The keys, when appropriate, immediately follow the puzzle or worksheet. Bingo cards immediately follow the bingo clues. There are two main groups of activities: one group for the unit; that is, generally relating to the *Farewell to Manzanar* text, and another group of activities related strictly to the *Farewell to Manzanar* vocabulary.

Directions for the games, puzzles, and worksheets are self-explanatory. The object here is to provide you with extra materials you may use in any way you choose.

MORE ACTIVITIES *Farewell to Manzanar*

1. Pick one of the incidents for students to dramatize. Encourage students to write dialog for the characters. (Perhaps you could assign various stories to different groups of students so more than one story could be acted and more students could participate.)

2. Have students design a bulletin board (ready to be put up; not just sketched) for *Farewell to Manzanar*.

3. Invite someone to talk to the class about survival in a resettlement camp.

4. If you live near a military base, you may be able to have someone from the base come and talk about their training in preparation for war.

5. Ask someone from the Society of Friends (Quakers) to talk about their efforts on behalf of the Japanese Americans in the resettlement camps during World War II.

6. Help students design and produce a talk show. Choose one of the story incidents as the topic. The host will interview the various characters. (Students should make up the questions they want the host to ask the characters.)

7. Have students work in pairs to create an interview with one of the characters. One student should be the interviewer and the other should be the interviewee. Students can work together to compose questions for the interviewer to ask. Each pair of students could present their interview to the class.

8. Invite students who have read other books by Jeanne Wakatsuki Houston and/or her husband, James Houston, to present booktalks to the class.

9. Invite students who have read other books on a similar topic as *Farewell to Manzanar* to present booktalks to the class.

10. Use some of the related topics (noted earlier for an in-class library) as topics for research, reports, or written papers, or as topics for guest speakers.

11. Invite someone who has lived in one of the areas mentioned in the book to speak to the class.

12. Have students hold small group discussions related to topics in the book. Assign a recorder and a speaker for each group. Have the speaker from each group make a report to the class.

MORE ACTIVITIES *Farewell to Manzanar*

13. Use the Internet to take a virtual field trip to the Manzanar National Historic Site, which is run by the National Park Service. The Web address is: http://www.nps-gov/manz/.

14. Research life of Japanese immigrants to the United States between 1869 and 1942.

15. Research the three Supreme Court cases mentioned in the book, as well as other related cases. Prepare a report for the class using a computer and presentation software.

16. If possible, speak with someone whose relatives or friends were detained at one of the camps and report on their experiences. (Note: Caution students to be sensitive if they do this activity.)

17. Bring in traditional Japanese music and play it for the class.

18. Write additional chapters for the book, telling what was happening in other parts of the United States during World War II.

19. Find out how Japanese-Americans live in the United States today.

20. There were ten resettlement camps for the Japanese Americans during World War II. Find out more about one of the other camps and make a presentation to the class.

21. Give each student one bingo card. Students should use all the words on their bingo cards in a composition about the novel.

WORD SEARCH 1 *Farewell to Manzanar*

```
T P K H E S T R A W B E R R I E S S E R G N O C S
N S G I M M Z N F P N C P X G G V F P R N S L Y N
A F T R I D M N X G V N N Q H Z L C P H Z N L Z L
I C C O G R T J V K H O K S T N A R G I M M I Q S
C Z W S R F N A D C C I C V Y P N W O O D Y R K T
I F D H A H P N T M P T F X N Y K Y L F Y V B K M
T L W I T R E O F T P A Z S W I Z S M C A K A M X
E Y P M I S S C X N A U K C Q M C L O M F M C M S
I H N A O T N E M A R C A S C O O P E R A T I V E
D N J J N W N A W W A A K R U T N Z E A C Z Q L M
X J U Z N I E N C R M V G T J A W W H N N H S T Y
S M W E N C J N R L X E S N P B E Q D A A K A E Z
V H V K A Z E A S J O E R A D I N E N Z S L O R F
V E I W W N B T Z Y D S J V V L Y E A N H F O M D
S S B G A M K N L C N P E R T L V C S A P B X I D
L L U C Y Z D M P T E Q E D F E I H U M R L N N B
O F D R X E T C E Q H T K Z L L S I O A G L A A C
Y Q D S R B X L X X N I M E O I P Z H D O L M L V
A X H F B E L L R I P M R H F F N U T C N B R L Y
L M I Y Q A N O Q M M O T T H X R T N I J S E D H
T V S G B H N D F G Y A T B Y C A I M L E X H C V
Y M T F D A S W E I C Y C N K B L S N S R H S L W
R Q U E E N L S K R K K L K M E N G L I S H I K G
X K J L N B F G F X D F K O H T W S C S E K F M Q
S N E Z I T I C E D U L C X E D I S L O Y A L T Y
```

ATTACK	COOPERATIVE	FRED	KO	SEVEN
BALLET	DIETICIAN	HARBOR	LINCOLN	SHIG
BARRACKS	DISLOYALTY	HIROSHIMA	LOYALTY	STRAWBERRIES
BILL	ELEANOR	IMMIGRANTS	MANZANAR	SURRENDER
BUDDHIST	ELEVEN	INLAND	NASH	TERMINAL
CABRILLO	EMIGRATION	INTERVIEWER	NINE	THIRTY
CANE	ENDO	INU	OCEAN	THOUSAND
CATHOLIC	ENGLISH	JAPAN	ORCHARD	TOMI
CHIZU	EVACUATION	JERSEY	OWENS	WOODY
CITIZENS	EXCLUDE	JOE	QUEEN	
CLOSED	FAMILY	JOSE	RADINE	
COMBAT	FISH	KAZ	SACRAMENTO	
CONGRESS	FISHERMAN	KIYO	SCOUTS	

ANSWER KEY WORD SEARCH 1 *Farewell to Manzanar*

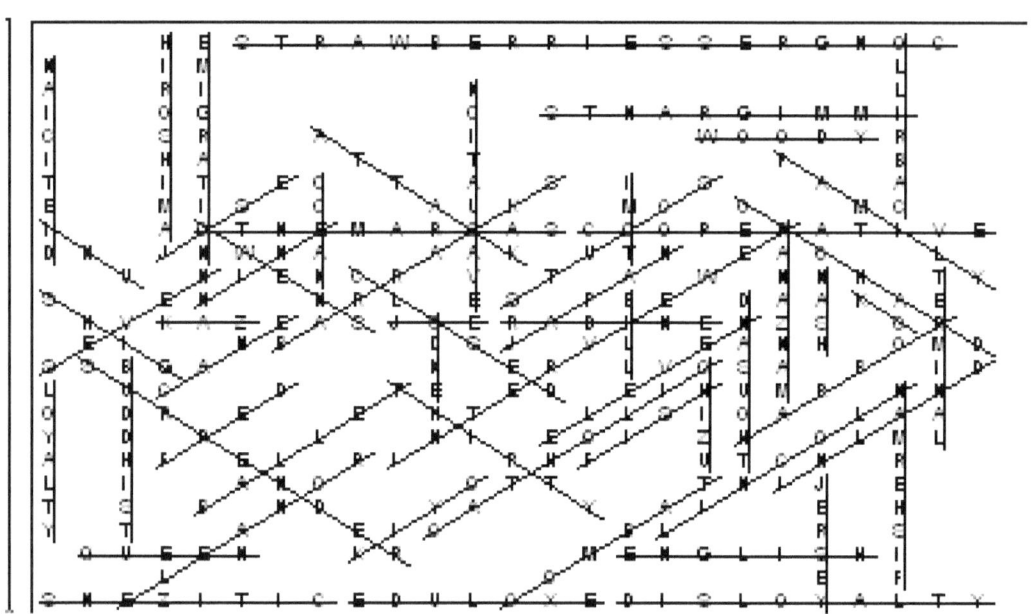

WORD SEARCH 2 *Farewell to*

Words are placed backwards, forward, diagonally, up and down. Words listed below are included in the maze. Circle the hidden vocabulary words in the maze.

```
S C S F I S H E R M A N O Z
H H D T H A N J W S N V W K
I I E P R I T D J C E M E R
G Z S B N A E C F O K F N X
V U O O F R W M J U X A S N
E R L R F I A B Z T Y M E T
X L C C B N S R E S E I V R
D G E H Z I O H N R S L E H
Y T L A Y O L S I D R Y N Q
R V N R N L L L D B E I P W
D A N D D O I F A C J N E Z
R T C K C C R N R W A O H S
W O O D Y N B O C E A N S L
K G M M A E A F Q O M Y E E
Q L B P I V C V O U L S N G
R K A Z N E M W Y W E N X K
H J T P U L A N I M R E T K
E N D O X E K O K H S A N M
```

BILL	ELEVEN	JAPAN	MANZANAR	
CABRILLO	ENDO	JERSEY	NASH	SEVEN
CANE	FAMILY	JOE	NINE	SHIG
CHIZU	FISH	JOSE	OCEAN	STRAWBERRIES
CLOSED	FISHERMAN	KAZ	ORCHARD	TERMINAL
COMBAT	FRED	KIYO	OWENS	TOMI
DISLOYALTY	HARBOR	KO	QUEEN	WOODY
ELEANOR	INU	LINCOLN	RADINE	SCOUTS

ANSWER KEY WORD SEARCH 2 *Farewell to Manzanar*

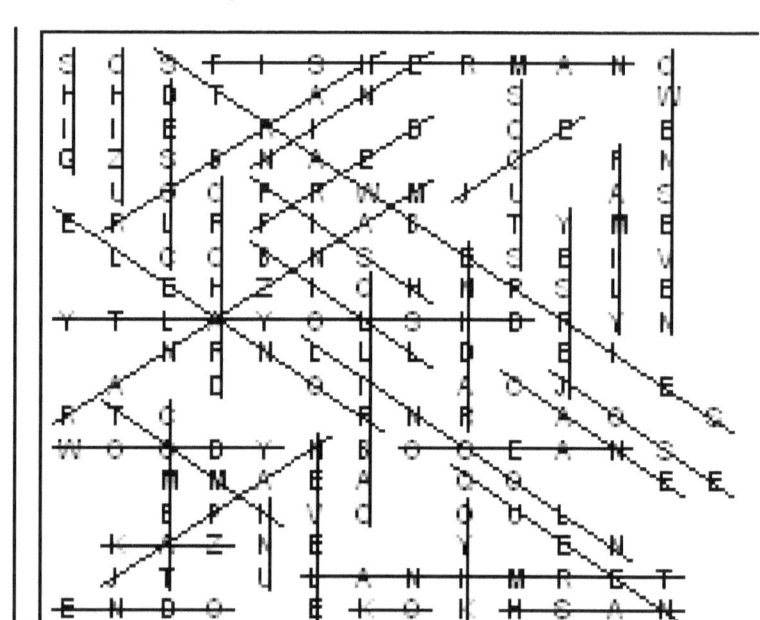

UNIT CROSSWORD PUZZLE 1 *Farewell to Manzanar*

CROSSWORD 1 CLUES *Farewell to Manzanar*

ACROSS

3 San___; family home for Jeanne's last year in high school
5 Mama's job at the camp
6 Ka-Ke; Papa's home in ____
7 ____ Park; where Wakatsuki family lived before their internment
13 Ft. ___; Papa was imprisoned there
15 Number of interned Japanese-Americans: 110 ____
17 Family's religion
19 Age of Jeanne's daughter when they went to the camp
21 Jeanne's brother; punched Papa in the face to protect Mama
22 Jeanne's older brother; led a dance-band; sent to Germany
24 Public Law 414 allowed Japanese-Americans to become US ____
28 Number of months Papa spent at Ft. Lincoln
33 Hirabayashi & Korematsu challenged racial bias of ____ order & lost
36 Traitor; women called Papa this
37 August 6, 1945 US dropped atom bomb on _____
38 Model of car Papa drove out of Manzanar
39 August 14, 1945 Japan ____ed; WWII ended

DOWN

1 Jeanne's age when the family went to Manzanar
2 Foreman of the reservoir crew
3 Mr. Kurihara; leader of the Manzanar camp riot
4 Mitsue ___ protested internment under habeas corpus & won
5 Greatest possible disgrace for a Japanese man to be charged with
6 Several of Jeanne's family members moved to New ___ after the war
7 ___ Valley, CA; location of Manzanar camp
8 December 7, 1941 was the date of the Japanese ___ on Pearl Harbor
9 Papa's job before internment
10 Papa's first name
11 Jeanne's older brother; drafted into US Army; visited Japan
12 Papa's job at Ft. Lincoln
14 ___ Homes; where the family lived after the war was over
16 Woody's wife
18 Bill's wife
20 Jeanne's older sister; re-entered camp; had a baby in camp
23 Oath Japanese-American men were asked to sign
24 Papa's version of the samurai sword
25 Number of years it took Jeanne to go back to Manzanar
26 Language Jeanne spoke
27 Eleanor's husband; drafted into US Army
29 Jeanne's elected position; Carnival ____
30 Girl ___ did not accept Jeanne as a member
31 Mess hall caused the disintegration of the ___
32 August 12, 1942 Evacuation to the ___ camps was completed
34 Mr. Tayama's first name; he was beaten at camp and almost died
35 Mama worked at the ___ cannery

ANSWER KEY UNIT CROSSWORD PUZZLE 1 *Farewell to Manzanar*

UNIT CROSSWORD PUZZLE 2 *Farewell to Manzanar*

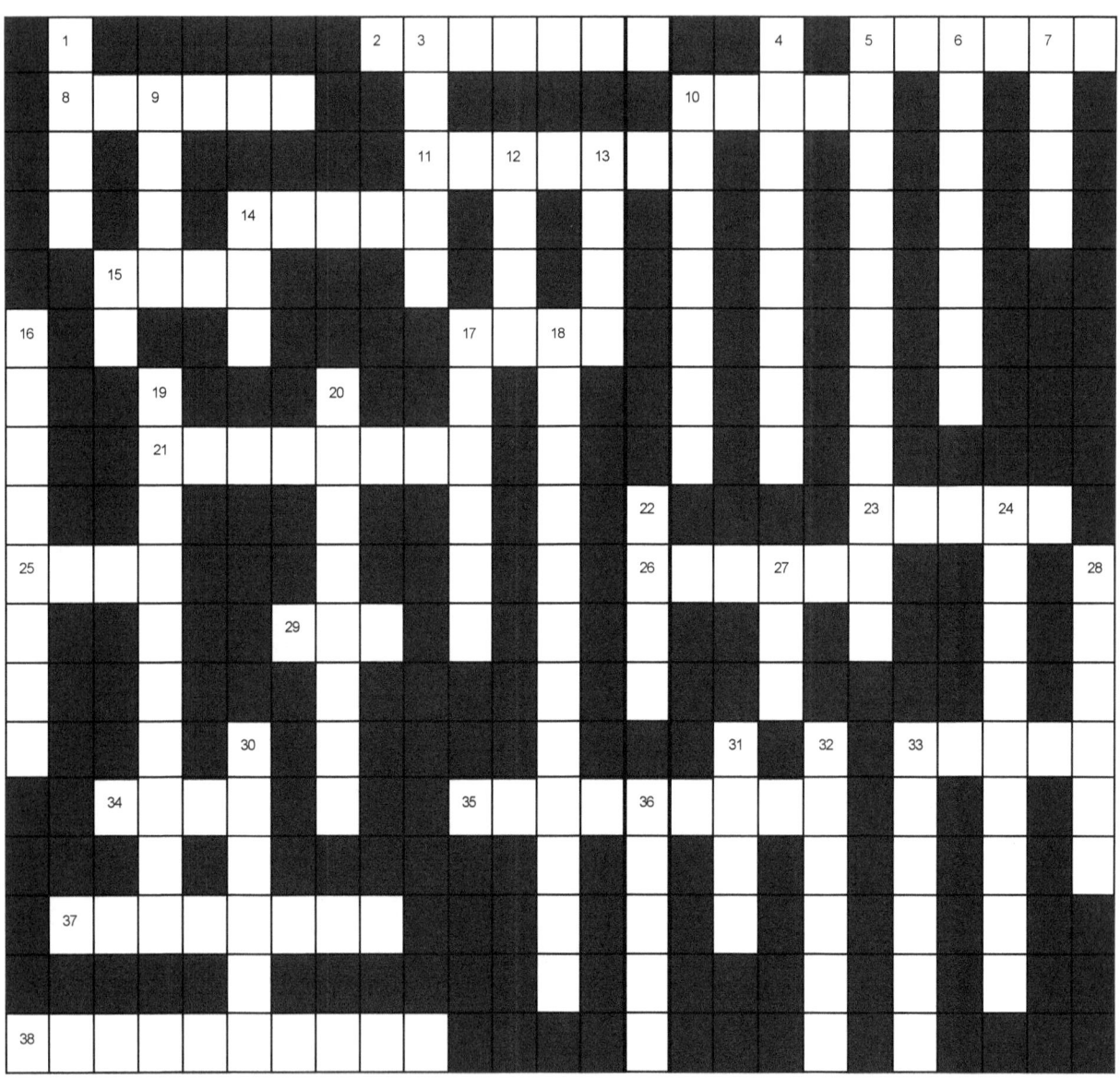

152

CLUES UNIT CROSSWORD 2 *Farewell to Manzanar*

ACROSS

2 Oath Japanese-American men were asked to sign
5 August 12, 1942 Evacuation to ten ___ camps was completed
8 December 7, 1941 was the date of the Japanese ___ on Pearl Harbor
10 ___ Park; where Wakatsuki family lived before their internment
11 Jeanne's older sister; re-entered camp; had a baby in camp
14 Ka-Ke; Papa's home in ___
15 Jeanne's older brother; punched Papa to protect Mama
17 San ___; family home for Jeanne's last year in high school
21 Resettlement camp for Japanese Americans
23 Jeanne's older brother; drafted into the US Army; visited Japan
25 Eleanor's husband; drafted into US Army
26 Jeanne's friend in junior high but not in high school
29 Foreman of the reservoir crew
33 Woody's wife
34 Mama worked at the ___ cannery
35 August 6, 1945 US dropped atom bomb on ___
37 In 1924 immigration from Japan was stopped by US ___
38 Greatest possible disgrace for a Japanese man to be charged with

DOWN

1 Papa's version of the samurai sword
3 ___ Valley, CA; location of Manzanar camp
4 Long Beach was the location of ___ Island
5 Papa's job at Ft. Lincoln
6 Ft. ___; Papa was imprisoned there
7 Model of car Papa drove out of Manzanar
9 Bill's wife
10 Spring of 1943 the family moved near the peach ___
12 Mitsue ___ protested internment under habeas corpus & won
13 Number of months Papa spent at Ft. Lincoln
14 Mr. Kurihara; leader of Manzanar camp riot
15 Papa's first name
16 Number of interned Japanese-Americans: 110 ___
17 Several of Jeanne's family members moved to New ___ after the war
18 In 1952 the family moved to San Jose and Papa raised ___
19 In 1886 the Japanese government lifted its ban on ___
12 Block 16 was the location of the first ___ the family lived in
22 Mr. Tayama's first name; he was beaten at camp and almost died
24 Mama's job at the camp
27 Traitor; women called Papa this
28 Girl ___ did not accept Jeanne as a member
30 Number of years it took Jeanne to go back to Manzanar
31 Jeanne's older brother; led a dance-band; sent to Germany
32 Mess hall caused the disintegration of the ___
33 December 5, 1945 Manzanar camp officially ___
36 Jeanne's age when the family went to Manzanar

ANSWER KEY UNIT CROSSWORD 2 *Farewell to Manzanar*

MATCHING QUIZ 1 *Farewell to Manzanar* Dates and Numbers

Directions: Place the letter of the matching definition on the blank line.

_____ 1. 1886   A. evacuation to ten inland camps is completed

_____ 2. 1869   B. U. S. drops atom bomb on Hiroshima

_____ 3. 1924   C. Jeanne's age when the family goes to Manzanar

_____ 4. 1952   D. Japanese government lifted its ban on emigration

_____ 5. Dec. 7, 1941   E. number of years before Jeanne went back to Manzanar

_____ 6. March 25, 1942   F. allowed Japanese-Americans to become U. S. citizens

_____ 7. Aug. 12, 1942   G. location of the first barracks the family lived in

_____ 8. Aug. 14, 1945   H. let military exclude people from Western areas

_____ 9. Spring of 1943   I. first Japanese immigrants arrive in U. S.

_____ 10. Aug. 6, 1945   J. number of months Papa spent at Fort Lincoln

_____ 11. Dec. 5, 1942   K. second "home" at Manzanar, larger quarters

_____ 12. April 1972   L. age of Jeanne's daughter when they went to the camp

_____ 13. 7   M. Public Law 414 is passed

_____ 14. 9   N. night of Manzanar camp riot

_____ 15. 11   O. family moves near the pear orchard

_____ 16. 30   P. Japanese attack Pearl Harbor

_____ 17. Block 16   Q. evacuees begin to arrive at Manzanar

_____ 18. Exec. Order 9066   R. immigration from Japan stopped by U. S. Congress

_____ 19. Public Law 414   S. Japan surrenders, WW II ends

_____ 20. Block 28   T. Jeanne traveled to Manzanar with family

ANSWER KEY MATCHING QUIZ 1 *Farewell to Manzanar* Dates and Numbers

D 1. 1886		A. evacuation to ten inland camps is completed
I 2. 1869		B. U. S. drops atom bomb on Hiroshima
R 3. 1924		C. Jeanne's age when the family goes to Manzanar
M 4. 1952		D. Japanese government lifted its ban on emigration
P 5. Dec. 7, 1941		E. number of years before Jeanne went back to Manzanar
Q 6. March 25, 1942		F. allowed Japanese-Americans to become U. S. citizens
A 7. Aug. 12, 1942		G. location of the first barracks the family lived in
S 8. Aug. 14, 1945		H. let military exclude people from Western areas
O 9. Spring of 1943		I. first Japanese immigrants arrive in U. S.
B 10. Aug. 6, 1945		J. number of months Papa spent at Fort Lincoln
N 11. Dec. 5, 1942		K. second "home" at Manzanar, larger quarters
T 12. April 1972		L. age of Jeanne's daughter when they went to the camp
C 13. 7		M. Public Law 414 is passed
J 14. 9		N. night of Manzanar camp riot
L 15. 11		O. family moves near the pear orchard
E 16. 30		P. Japanese attack Pearl Harbor
G 17. Block 16		Q. evacuees begin to arrive at Manzanar
H 18. Exec. Order 9066		R. immigration from Japan stopped by U. S. Congress
F 19. Public Law 414		S. Japan surrenders, WW II ends
K 20. Block 28		T. Jeanne traveled to Manzanar with family

MATCHING QUIZ 2 *Farewell to Manzanar* People and Places

Directions: Place the letter of the matching definition on the blank line.

_____ 1. Pearl Harbor   A. California, location of Manzanar camp

_____ 2. Long Beach   B. leader of Manzanar camp riot

_____ 3. Terminal Island   C. punched Papa in the face to protect Mama

_____ 4. Ocean Park   D. Jeanne's brother; oldest son; led a dance band

_____ 5. Fort Lincoln   E. protested internment under *habeas corpus*; won case

_____ 6. Owens Valley   F. fishing boats left from dock here

_____ 7. Ka-ke   G. Jeanne's brother-in-law, foreman of the reservoir crew

_____ 8. Cabrillo Homes   H. Jeanne's brother; in U.S. Army, visited Japan

_____ 9. Radine   I. challenged racial bias of evacuation order and civil rights

_____ 10. New Jersey   J. L. A. area, family home after the war was over

_____ 11. Ko Wakatsuki   K. challenged racial bias of evacuation; lost case

_____ 12. Bill Wakatsuki   L. Papa was imprisoned there

_____ 13. Joe Kurihara   M. Papa's full name

_____ 14. Woody Wakatsuki   N. California, location of Terminal Island

_____ 15. Fred Tayama   O. several family members moved here after war

_____ 16. Kiyo Wakatsuki   P. American base in Hawaii bombed by Japan in WW II

_____ 17. Kaz   Q. Jeanne's white friend in junior high but not high school

_____ 18. Gordon Hirabayashi R. Wakatsuki family home before internment

_____ 19. Fred Korematsu   S. beaten at camp and almost died

_____ 20. Mitsue Endo   T. Papa's home in Japan, near Hiroshima

ANSWER KEY MATCHING QUIZ 2 *Farewell to Manzanar* People and Places

P 1. Pearl Harbor   A. California, location of Manzanar camp

N 2. Long Beach   B. leader of Manzanar camp riot

F 3. Terminal Island   C. punched Papa in the face to protect Mama

R 4. Ocean Park   D. Jeanne's brother; oldest son; led a dance band

L 5. Fort Lincoln   E. protested internment under *habeas corpus*; won case

A 6. Owens Valley   F. fishing boats left from dock here

T 7. Ka-ke   G. Jeanne's brother-in-law, foreman of the reservoir crew

J 8. Cabrillo Homes   H. Jeanne's brother; in U.S. Army, visited Japan

Q 9. Radine   I. challenged racial bias of evacuation order and civil rights

O 10. New Jersey   J. L. A. area, family home after the war was over

M 11. Ko Wakatsuki   K. challenged racial bias of evacuation; lost case

D 12. Bill Wakatsuki   L. Papa was imprisoned there

B 13. Joe Kurihara   M. Papa's full name

H 14. Woody Wakatsuki   N. California, location of Terminal Island

S 15. Fred Tayama   O. several of family members moved here after war

C 16. Kiyo Wakatsuki   P. American base in Hawaii bombed by Japan in WW II

G 17. Kaz   Q. Jeanne's white friend in junior high but not high school

I 18. Gordon Hirabayashi   R. Wakatsuki family home before internment

K 19. Fred Korematsu   S. beaten at camp and almost died

E 20. Mitsue Endo   T. Papa's home in Japan, near Hiroshima

JUGGLE LETTER 1 - Farewell to Manzanar

1. NQUEE = 1. _____
   Jeanne's elected position; Carnival _____

2. OK = 2. _____
   Papa's first name

3. ATIEMRLN = 3. _____
   Long Beach was the location of _____ Island

4. KTAACT = 4. _____
   December 7, 1941 was the date of the Japanese _____ on Pearl Harbor

5. CTDNIEIIA = 5. _____
   Mama's job at the camp

6. TZCNESII = 6. _____
   Public Law 414 allowed Japanese-Americans to become US _____

7. AARMANZN = 7. _____
   Resettlement camp for Japanese Americans

8. MFNSEIHRA = 8. _____
   Papa's job before internment

9. YIKO = 9. _____
   Jeanne's brother; punched Papa in the face to protect Mama

10. VUATCEIOAN =10. _____
    Hirabayashi & Korematsu challenged racial bias of _____ order & lost

11. ANAJP =11. _____
    Ka-Ke; Papa's home in _____

12. IHTTRY =12. _____
    Number of years it took Jeanne to go back to Manzanar

13. AKRSABCR =13. _____
    Block 16 was the location of the first ____ the family lived in

14. YERJSE =14. _____
    Several of Jeanne's family members moved to New ___ after the war

15. HUICZ =15. _____
Woody's wife

16. EREVENTIWRI =16. _____
Papa's job at Ft. Lincoln

17. DRFE =17. _____
Mr. Tayama's first name; he was beaten at camp and almost died

18. MFYAIL =18. _____
Mess hall caused the disintegration of the _____

19. LEAOENR =19. _____
Jeanne's older sister; re-entered camp; had a baby in camp

20. TINAMGSIMR =20. _____
In 1869 the first Japanese ____ arrived in the US

21. GHSI =21. _____
Eleanor's husband; drafted into US Army

22. AOCEN =22. _____
____ Park; where Wakatsuki family lived before their internment

23. AREIIMTGNO =23. _____
in 1886 the Japanese government lifted its ban on _____

24. TSDUHIDB =24. _____
Family's religion

25. ILDTYASYLO =25. _____
Greatest possible disgrace for a Japanese man to be charged with

26. ELTABL =26. _____
Jeanne thought it was a misuse of the body

27. LDOCSE =27. _____
December 5, 1945 Manzanar camp officially _____

28. OYTALYL =28. _____
Oath Japanese-American men were asked to sign

29. MROIHHAIS =29. _____
August 6, 1945 US dropped atom bomb on _____

JUGGLE LETTER ANSWER KEY 1 - Farewell to Manzanar

1. NQUEE = 1. QUEEN
   Jeanne's elected position; Carnival _____

2. OK = 2. KO
   Papa's first name

3. ATIEMRLN = 3. TERMINAL
   Long Beach was the location of _____ Island

4. KTAACT = 4. ATTACK
   December 7, 1941 was the date of the Japanese _____ on Pearl Harbor

5. CTDNIEIIA = 5. DIETICIAN
   Mama's job at the camp

6. TZCNESII = 6. CITIZENS
   Public Law 414 allowed Japanese-Americans to become US _____

7. AARMANZN = 7. MANZANAR
   Resettlement camp for Japanese Americans

8. MFNSEIHRA = 8. FISHERMAN
   Papa's job before internment

9. YIKO = 9. KIYO
   Jeanne's brother; punched Papa in the face to protect Mama

10. VUATCEIOAN = 10. EVACUATION
    Hirabayashi & Korematsu challenged racial bias of _____ order & lost

11. ANAJP = 11. JAPAN
    Ka-Ke; Papa's home in _____

12. IHTTRY = 12. THIRTY
    Number of years it took Jeanne to go back to Manzanar

13. AKRSABCR = 13. BARRACKS
    Block 16 was the location of the first _____ the family lived in

14. YERJSE = 14. JERSEY
    Several of Jeanne's family members moved to New _____ after the war

15. HUICZ =15. CHIZU
Woody's wife

16. EREVENTIWRI =16. INTERVIEWER
Papa's job at Ft. Lincoln

17. DRFE =17. FRED
Mr. Tayama's first name; he was beaten at camp and almost died

18. MFYAIL =18. FAMILY
Mess hall caused the disintegration of the _____

19. LEAOENR =19. ELEANOR
Jeanne's older sister; re-entered camp; had a baby in camp

20. TINAMGSIMR =20. IMMIGRANTS
In 1869 the first Japanese ____ arrived in the US

21. GHSI =21. SHIG
Eleanor's husband; drafted into US Army

22. AOCEN =22. OCEAN
____ Park; where Wakatsuki family lived before their internment

23. AREIIMTGNO =23. EMIGRATION
in 1886 the Japanese government lifted its ban on _____

24. TSDUHIDB =24. BUDDHIST
Family's religion

25. ILDTYASYLO =25. DISLOYALTY
Greatest possible disgrace for a Japanese man to be charged with

26. ELTABL =26. BALLET
Jeanne thought it was a misuse of the body

27. LDOCSE =27. CLOSED
December 5, 1945 Manzanar camp officially _____

28. OYTALYL =28. LOYALTY
Oath Japanese-American men were asked to sign

29. MROIHHAIS =29. HIROSHIMA
August 6, 1945 US dropped atom bomb on _____

JUGGLE LETTER 2 - Farewell to Manzanar

1. GNORCESS = 1. _____
   In 1924 immigration from Japan was stopped by US _____

2. RROBAH = 2. _____
   Pearl ___; American base in Hawaii bombed by Japan

3. SISEBWREARRT = 3. _____
   In 1952 the family moved to San Jose and Papa raised _____

4. MOIT = 4. _____
   Bill's wife

5. HNAS = 5. _____
   Model of car Papa drove out of Manzanar

6. NLLONCI = 6. _____
   Ft. ___; Papa was imprisoned there

7. TIOEACVREOP = 7. _____
   Papa drafted plans to start one but never started it

8. IRADEN = 8. _____
   Jeanne's friend in junior high but not high school

9. SANETMAROC = 9. _____
   California city where first Japanese immigrants settled

10. SOEJ =10. _____
    San ___; family home for Jeanne's last year in high school

11. EVESN =11. _____
    Jeanne's age when the family went to Manzanar

12. ANEC =12. _____
    Papa's version of the samurai sword

13. ZKA =13. _____
    Foreman of the reservoir crew

14. IHSF =14. _____
    Mama worked at the ___ cannery

15. DOWOY =15. _____
    Jeanne's older brother; drafted into the US Army; visited Japan

16. TSSOCU =16. _____

Girl ___ did not accept Jeanne as a member

17. OEDN =17. _____

Mitsue ___ protested internment under habeas corpus & won

18. UDECXEL =18. _____

Executive Order 9066 allowed the military to _____ people from Western areas

19. NILNDA =19. _____

August 12, 1942 Evacuation to ten ____ camps was completed

20. DUNSOHAT =20. _____

Number of interned Japanese-Americans: 110 _____

21. EINN =21. _____

Number of months Papa spent at Ft. Lincoln

22. OJE =22. _____

Mr. Kurihara; leader of Manzanar camp riot

23. AODHCRR =23. _____

Spring of 1943 the family moved near the peach ____

24. HNSIELG =24. _____

Language Jeanne spoke

25. LBLI =25. _____

Jeanne's older brother; led a dance-band; sent to Germany

26. OHAITCCL =26. _____

Religion to which Jeanne wanted to convert

27. EWNSO =27. _____

____ Valley, CA; location of Manzanar camp

28. EVNELE =28. _____

Age of Jeanne's daughter when they went to the camp

29. UNI =29. _____

Traitor; women called Papa this

JUGGLE LETTER ANSWER KEY 2 - Farewell to Manzanar
JUGGLE WITH CLUES

1. GNORCESS = 1. CONGRESS
   In 1924 immigration from Japan was stopped by US _____

2. RROBAH = 2. HARBOR
   Pearl ___; American base in Hawaii bombed by Japan

3. SISEBWREARRT = 3. STRAWBERRIES
   In 1952 the family moved to San Jose and Papa raised _____

4. MOIT = 4. TOMI
   Bill's wife

5. HNAS = 5. NASH
   Model of car Papa drove out of Manzanar

6. NLLONCI = 6. LINCOLN
   Ft. ____; Papa was imprisoned there

7. TIOEACVREOP = 7. COOPERATIVE
   Papa drafted plans to start one but never started it

8. IRADEN = 8. RADINE
   Jeanne's friend in junior high but not high school

9. SANETMAROC = 9. SACRAMENTO
   California city where first Japanese immigrants settled

10. SOEJ = 10. JOSE
    San ____; family home for Jeanne's last year in high school

11. EVESN = 11. SEVEN
    Jeanne's age when the family went to Manzanar

12. ANEC = 12. CANE
    Papa's version of the samurai sword

13. ZKA = 13. KAZ
    Foreman of the reservoir crew

14. IHSF = 14. FISH
    Mama worked at the ___ cannery

15. DOWOY = 15. WOODY
    Jeanne's older brother; drafted into the US Army; visited Japan

16. TSSOCU =16. SCOUTS
Girl ___ did not accept Jeanne as a member

17. OEDN =17. ENDO
Mitsue ___ protested internment under habeas corpus & won

18. UDECXEL =18. EXCLUDE
Executive Order 9066 allowed the military to _____ people from Western areas

19. NILNDA =19. INLAND
August 12, 1942 Evacuation to ten ____ camps was completed

20. DUNSOHAT =20. THOUSAND
Number of interned Japanese-Americans: 110 _____

21. EINN =21. NINE
Number of months Papa spent at Ft. Lincoln

22. OJE =22. JOE
Mr. Kurihara; leader of Manzanar camp riot

23. AODHCRR =23. ORCHARD
Spring of 1943 the family moved near the peach ____

24. HNSIELG =24. ENGLISH
Language Jeanne spoke

25. LBLI =25. BILL
Jeanne's older brother; led a dance-band; sent to Germany

26. OHAITCCL =26. CATHOLIC
Religion to which Jeanne wanted to convert

27. EWNSO =27. OWENS
____ Valley, CA; location of Manzanar camp

28. EVNELE =28. ELEVEN
Age of Jeanne's daughter when they went to the camp

29. UNI =29. INU
Traitor; women called Papa this

WORD LIST Farewell to Manzanar

ATTACK	December 7, 1941 was the date of the Japanese _____ on Pearl Harbor
BALLET	Jeanne thought it was a misuse of the body
BARRACKS	Block 16 was the location of the first ____ the family lived in
BILL	Jeanne's older brother; led a dance-band; sent to Germany
BUDDHIST	Family's religion
CABRILLO	____ Homes; where the family lived after the war was over
CANE	Papa's version of the samurai sword
CATHOLIC	Religion to which Jeanne wanted to convert
CHIZU	Woody's wife
CITIZENS	Public Law 414 allowed Japanese-Americans to become US _____
CLOSED	December 5, 1945 Manzanar camp officially _____
COMBAT	442nd ____ Regiment was an all nisei unit in the US Army
CONGRESS	In 1924 immigration from Japan was stopped by US _____
COOPERATIVE	Papa drafted plans to start one but never started it
DIETICIAN	Mama's job at the camp
DISLOYALTY	Greatest possible disgrace for a Japanese man to be charged with
ELEANOR	Jeanne's older sister; re-entered camp; had a baby in camp
ELEVEN	Age of Jeanne's daughter when they went to the camp
EMIGRATION	In 1886 the Japanese government lifted its ban on _____
ENDO	Mitsue ___ protested internment under habeas corpus & won
ENGLISH	Language Jeanne spoke
EVACUATION	Hirabayashi & Korematsu challenged racial bias of _____ order & lost
EXCLUDE	Executive Order 9066 allowed the military to _____ people from Western areas
FAMILY	Mess hall caused the disintegration of the _____
FISH	Mama worked at the ___ cannery
FISHERMAN	Papa's job before internment
FRED	Mr. Tayama's first name; he was beaten at camp and almost died
HARBOR	Pearl ___; American base in Hawaii bombed by Japan
HIROSHIMA	August 6, 1945 US dropped atom bomb on _____
IMMIGRANTS	In 1869 the first Japanese ____ arrived in the US
INLAND	August 12, 1942 Evacuation to ten ____ camps was completed
INTERVIEWER	Papa's job at Ft. Lincoln
INU	Traitor; women called Papa this
JAPAN	Ka-Ke; Papa's home in _____
JERSEY	Several of Jeanne's family members moved to New ___ after the war
JOE	Mr. Kurihara; leader of Manzanar camp riot
JOSE	San ____; family home for Jeanne's last year in high school

Farewell to Manzanar Word List Continued

KAZ	Foreman of the reservoir crew
KIYO	Jeanne's brother; punched Papa in the face to protect Mama
KO	Papa's first name
LINCOLN	Ft. ____; Papa was imprisoned there
LOYALTY	Oath Japanese-American men were asked to sign
MANZANAR	Resettlement camp for Japanese Americans
NASH	Model of car Papa drove out of Manzanar
NINE	Number of months Papa spent at Ft. Lincoln
OCEAN	____ Park; where Wakatsuki family lived before their internment
ORCHARD	Spring of 1943 the family moved near the peach ____
OWENS	____ Valley, CA; location of Manzanar camp
QUEEN	Jeanne's elected position; Carnival ____
RADINE	Jeanne's friend in junior high but not high school
SACRAMENTO	California city where first Japanese immigrants settled
SCOUTS	Girl ____ did not accept Jeanne as a member
SEVEN	Jeanne's age when the family went to Manzanar
SHIG	Eleanor's husband; drafted into US Army
STRAWBERRIES	In 1952 the family moved to San Jose and Papa raised ____
SURRENDER	August 14, 1945 Japan _____ed; WWII ended
TERMINAL	Long Beach was the location of ____ Island
THIRTY	Number of years it took Jeanne to go back to Manzanar
THOUSAND	Number of interned Japanese-Americans: 110 ____
TOMI	Bill's wife
WOODY	Jeanne's older brother; drafted into the US Army; visited Japan

VOCABULARY RESOURCE MATERIALS

VOCABULARY WORD SEARCH 1 *Farewell to Manzanar*

```
B E N E V O L E N T A I M P A C T D R E D G E Q
P Y C U D C R I N G E F S V E N T U R E N W C M
N X R Q Q I E C N A T S F S S E L E L I U G I N
J I E S S I C S E D A T E I U D W I N D L E Q G
Y E D E Y H N T G S W C F P R E H E P R S X W Y
Y T O T M S A P S H S I L Q Z M E G H I T E W C
L A G O C N N Y C N E T O P L R E D N O R C A T
V L O R U F E H P K K N U B A S S D O V O N L P
E I U G B M T T X O Q E R C G U Q F I R U A I D
C M G P I Q S L W B S H I T S O H S V E G N E J
N I I C I U G A S F T S C U U U Z I S H I N V
E S N F L M S R E K N U H T U R B U L E N T S K
C S G A E A R L G B O A A U P G M W B R Y S F S
S A E N S A N N N O Z S L M N O O O T G B L W
E D N B C U I T I S F F U C N O J B I Q M O Z D
I O L K I D B M E I E S N A S C U R E L I G I V
U V S I R A O D L N W V D R C N O S G L G N T N
Q E W A V H S I U Y J B E J H I D E N G I S E R
C R W R X I A K D E K S R Z R G Q V I M B S J Y
A T D D B L D R T Q D T J P S A B O T E U R K L
```

ACQUIESCENCE	CRINGE	IMPACT	POTENCY	TINGE
AFFIRMED	CUBICLES	INCONGRUOUS	PRIORITY	TROUGH
ALIENS	DREDGE	ISSEI	RESERVOIR	TURBULENT
ASSIMILATE	DWINDLE	ISSUE	RESIGNED	TURMOIL
ASUNDER	EDICTS	LIVID	SABOTEUR	VENTURE
AUTHENTIC	FILIAL	NISEI	SANSEI	VIGIL
BARRACKS	FLOURISH	OBELISK	SEDATE	VIGILANTE
BENEVOLENT	GOUGING	OBLIVION	SPASM	WARDING
BIAS	GROTESQUE	OBSTINANCE	STANCE	
CAREENING	GUILELESS	OMINOUS	SUBDUED	
CHAOS	HUNKER	OVERT	SURPLUS	
CREDO	IDEALIST	POSTHUMOUS	SUSTENANCE	

VOCABULARY WORD SEARCH 2 *Farewell to Manzanar*

```
R E S I G N E D O B S T I N A N C E G C
G X O B E L I S K T S I L A E D I D R B
H H Z V C F J W A C U C R I N G E I O T
E R U T N E V A U Y R R I J K S L C T Y
C A N P A G D R T R V E M C H N S T E Q
Y S G K N T U D H W S N D O N E S S S Z
M T J I E E N I E I B E S O I I U N Q E
V O L I T I O N N O I T A D I L A V U D
S R K O S A F G T J A A Q S P A I S E N
J A B D U P T N I N S D S R L G S N H H
C A N X S Z R I C F S E U E I I O L G V
S P A S M D E E N O I S G L D O V U G H
H U N K E R V B A G Q N V Y R R O I B B
V C Q N Y I O H K F I L I A L R X C D S
D C K G K Y C N E T O P M M T C A P M I
```

AGITATING	FILIAL	MAROONED	SANSEI	TURMOIL
ALIENS	GROTESQUE	NISEI	SEDATE	VALIDATION
AUTHENTIC	HUNKER	OBELISK	SPASM	VENTURE
BIAS	IDEALIST	OBSTINANCE	STANCE	VIGIL
CHAOS	IMPACT	OVERT	SURPLUS	VOLITION
CREDO	ISSEI	POTENCY	SUSTENANCE	
CRINGE	ISSUE	RESIGNED	TINGE	WARDING
EDICTS	LIVID	SABOTEUR	TROUGH	

ANSWER KEY VOCABULARY WORD SEARCH 1 *Farewell to Manzanar*

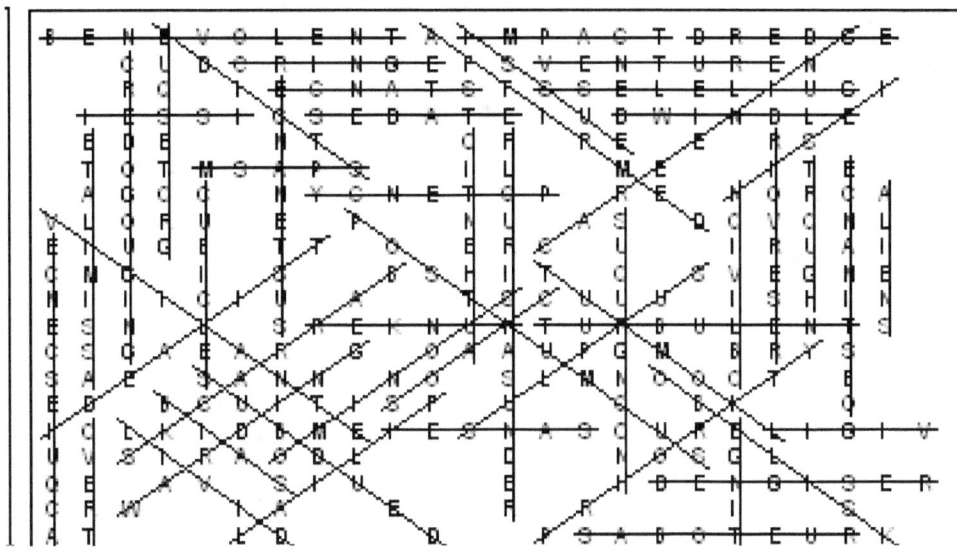

ANSWER KEY VOCABULARY WORD SEARCH 2 *Farewell to Manzanar*

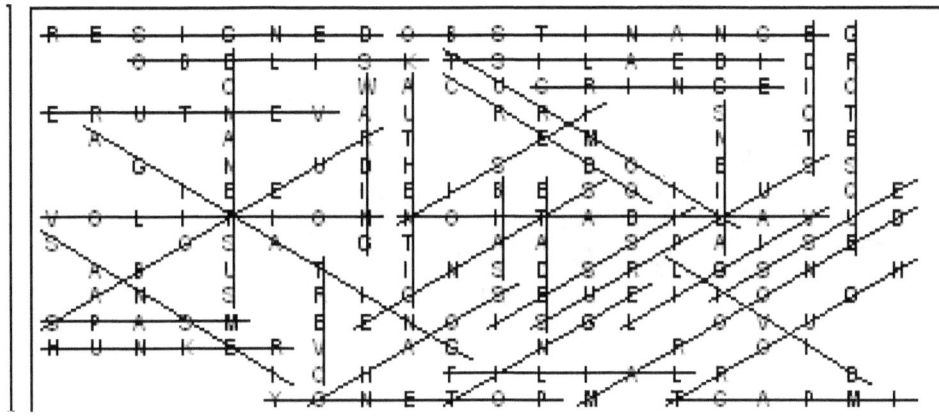

VOCABULARY CROSSWORD 1 *Farewell to Manzanar*

VOCABULARY CROSSWORD 1 CLUES *Farewell to Manzanar*

ACROSS

2 Large, plain buildings used for temporary housing
6 First generation; born in Japan
7 Stirring up public awareness and feeling
11 In pieces or separate parts
15 Public; not hidden
16 Beliefs
17 Agreement without objection
19 State of agitation or disturbance
22 Tapering, four-sided structure with a pyramid-shaped top
23 Honest, straightforward
26 Rules proclaimed by one in authority
29 Squat; sit back on one's heels
30 Unfavorable; threatening
31 Bring up
32 Second generation; Japanese born in US before WWII

DOWN

1 Going away in different directions
2 Preference based on prejudice
3 Person who harms an enemy nation
4 Manner of standing
5 Out of place
8 Forceful effect
9 Real; genuine
10 Kindly; charitable
12 Complete; without lines or restrictions
13 Make or become smaller or fewer
14 Canceled
16 Surrender on certain conditions
17 Declared to be true
18 Crouch in fear
19 A slight coloring
20 A showy display
21 Digging; tearing out
24 Extremely angry
25 Third generation; Japanese born in US after WWII
27 Matter or point of discussion
28 Involuntary muscle contraction

ANSWER KEY VOCABULARY CROSSWORD 1 *Farewell to Manzanar*

VOCABULARY CROSSWORD 2 *Farewell to Manzanar*

VOCABULARY CROSSWORD 2 CLUES *Farewell to Manzanar*

ACROSS

1 State of agitation or disturbance
4 Tapering, four-sided structure with a pyramid-shaped top
6 Forceful effect
9 Out of place
15 Calm, serious
17 Preference based on prejudice
18 First generation; born in Japan
23 Real; genuine
26 Squat; sit back on one's heels
28 Coming in order of importance
29 Bring up
31 One who wants things to be perfect
32 Involuntary muscle contraction
33 Public; not hidden
34 Of a son or daughter
35 Manner of standing

DOWN

1 Narrow, open container holding water
2 Accepting what comes without complaint
3 Extremely angry
5 Extra
7 Non-citizens of a living in a country
8 A slight coloring
10 Beliefs
11 Second generation; Japanese born in US before WWII
12 Stubbornness
13 Person who harms an enemy nation
14 In pieces or separate parts
16 Stirring up public awareness and feeling
19 Dare to go
20 Watching
21 Great confusion and disorder
22 Being forced to stay in a place
24 Violent
25 Overcome by force; conquered
27 Rules proclaimed by one in authority
28 Peacemaker
30 Make or become smaller or fewer
31 Matter or point of discussion

ANSWER KEY VOCABULARY CROSSWORD 2 *Farewell to Manzanar*

VOCABULARY MATCHING 1 - Farewell to Manzanar

___ 1. CAPITULATE
___ 2. TINGE
___ 3. PATRIARCH
___ 4. AFFIRMED
___ 5. CRINGE
___ 6. AGITATING
___ 7. COLLABORATOR
___ 8. SANSEI
___ 9. CONGESTION
___10. EDICTS
___11. RESERVOIR
___12. RESCINDED
___13. TROUGH
___14. INTERNMENT
___15. VALIDATION
___16. OBSTINANCE
___17. RESIGNED
___18. FLOURISH
___19. DREDGE
___20. ASUNDER
___21. SURPLUS
___22. PLACATOR
___23. GUILELESS
___24. INTANGIBLE
___25. HUNKER

A. Rules proclaimed by one in authority
B. Third generation; Japanese born in US after WWII
C. Extra
D. Crouch in fear
E. Squat; sit back on one's heels
F. A showy display
G. Male head of family
H. Confirmation; support by facts
I. One who cooperates treasonably, as with an enemy occupying one's country
J. Surrender on certain conditions
K. Stubbornness
L. Declared to be true
M. Stirring up public awareness and feeling
N. Accepting what comes without complaint
O. Canceled
P. Peacemaker
Q. Not able to be seen or touched
R. Place where water is collected and stored
S. In pieces or separate parts
T. Bring up
U. Being forced to stay in a place
V. Honest; straightforward
W. Narrow, open container holding water
X. An over-crowded condition
Y. A slight coloring

VOCABULARY MATCHING ANSWER KEY 1 - Farewell to Manzanar

J - 1. CAPITULATE		A. Rules proclaimed by one in authority
Y - 2. TINGE		B. Third generation; Japanese born in US after WWII
G - 3. PATRIARCH		C. Extra
L - 4. AFFIRMED		D. Crouch in fear
D - 5. CRINGE		E. Squat; sit back on one's heels
M - 6. AGITATING		F. A showy display
I - 7. COLLABORATOR		G. Male head of family
B - 8. SANSEI		H. Confirmation; support by facts
X - 9. CONGESTION		I. One who cooperates treasonably, as with an enemy occupying one's country
A -10. EDICTS		J. Surrender on certain conditions
R -11. RESERVOIR		K. Stubbornness
O -12. RESCINDED		L. Declared to be true
W 13. TROUGH		M. Stirring up public awareness and feeling
U -14. INTERNMENT		N. Accepting what comes without complaint
H -15. VALIDATION		O. Canceled
K -16. OBSTINANCE		P. Peacemaker
N -17. RESIGNED		Q. Not able to be seen or touched
F -18. FLOURISH		R. Place where water is collected and stored
T -19. DREDGE		S. In pieces or separate parts
S -20. ASUNDER		T. Bring up
C -21. SURPLUS		U. Being forced to stay in a place
P -22. PLACATOR		V. Honest; straightforward
V -23. GUILELESS		W. Narrow, open container holding water
Q -24. INTANGIBLE		X. An over-crowded condition
E -25. HUNKER		Y. A slight coloring

VOCABULARY MATCHING 2 - Farewell to Manzanar

___ 1. ISSEI   A. Unavoidable

___ 2. OMINOUS   B. In an arrogant, domineering way

___ 3. METAMORPHOSIS   C. Squat; sit back on one's heels

___ 4. CONFISCATORS   D. Unfavorable; threatening

___ 5. IMPERIOUSLY   E. First generation; born in Japan

___ 6. IMPACT   F. Forceful effect

___ 7. LIVID   G. Coming in order of importance

___ 8. VOLITION   H. Being open to attack or injury

___ 9. FLOURISH   I. A showy display

___10. EDICTS   J. Complete; without lines or restrictions

___11. SEDATE   K. Narrow, open container holding water

___12. VULNERABILITY   L. Keeping away

___13. TROUGH   M. Power; strength

___14. PRIORITY   N. Someone who takes the law into his own hands

___15. MAROONED   O. Decision or choice

___16. INEVITABLE   P. Matter or point of discussion

___17. TINGE   Q. Left in a helpless condition

___18. VIGILANTE   R. Rules proclaimed by one in authority

___19. BARRACKS   S. Become like the others in custom, etc.

___20. POTENCY   T. Large, plain buildings used for temporary housing

___21. HUNKER   U. A slight coloring

___22. UNQUALIFIED   V. Calm, serious

___23. ASSIMILATE   W. Extremely angry

___24. WARDING   X. Change of form or structure

___25. ISSUE   Y. Authorities who take and keep things

VOCABULARY MATCHING ANSWER KEY 2 - Farewell to Manzanar

E - 1. ISSEI	A.	Unavoidable
D - 2. OMINOUS	B.	In an arrogant, domineering way
X - 3. METAMORPHOSIS	C.	Squat; sit back on one's heels
Y - 4. CONFISCATORS	D.	Unfavorable; threatening
B - 5. IMPERIOUSLY	E.	First generation; born in Japan
F - 6. IMPACT	F.	Forceful effect
W - 7. LIVID	G.	Coming in order of importance
O - 8. VOLITION	H.	Being open to attack or injury
I - 9. FLOURISH	I.	A showy display
R -10. EDICTS	J.	Complete; without lines or restrictions
V -11. SEDATE	K.	Narrow, open container holding water
H -12. VULNERABILITY	L.	Keeping away
K -13. TROUGH	M.	Power; strength
G -14. PRIORITY	N.	Someone who takes the law into his own hands
Q -15. MAROONED	O.	Decision or choice
A -16. INEVITABLE	P.	Matter or point of discussion
U -17. TINGE	Q.	Left in a helpless condition
N -18. VIGILANTE	R.	Rules proclaimed by one in authority
T -19. BARRACKS	S.	Become like the others in custom, etc.
M -20. POTENCY	T.	Large, plain buildings used for temporary housing
C -21. HUNKER	U.	A slight coloring
J -22. UNQUALIFIED	V.	Calm, serious
S -23. ASSIMILATE	W.	Extremely angry
L -24. WARDING	X.	Change of form or structure
P -25. ISSUE	Y.	Authorities who take and keep things

VOCABULARY REVIEW SCRAMBLE 1 *Farewell to Manzanar*
Change the order of the letters to find the original word.

1. BCLCUEIS   1. C_____
                      Very small rooms

2. ETVRO   2. O_____
                      Public; not hidden

3. NSIAEL   3. A_____
                      Non-citizens living in a country

4. OAMTNRGIIE   4. E_____
                      Resettling in another country

5. URKNEH   5. H_____
                      Squat; sit back on one's heels

6. OCAFSRINTOSC   6. C_____
                      Authorities who take and keep things

7. RBESUOAT   7. S_____
                      Person who harms an enemy nation

8. SCNTEOIABN   8. O_____
                      Stubbornness

9. UROOUNGNCIS   9. I_____
                      Out of place

10. TASMLIEISA   10. A_____
                      Become like the others in custom, etc.

11. DGNIWAR   11. W_____
                      Keeping away

12. NERNEGCIA   12. C_____
                      Rushing headlong with a swaying motion

13. RTGHUO   13. T_____
                      Narrow, open container holding water

14. ARATITONIALZNU 14. N_____
                      Admitted to citizenship

15. AAIHTRPRC   15. P_____
                      Male head of family

16. EATTNHUCI   16. A_____
                      Real; genuine

17. EQCENEUCASIC   17. A_____
                      Agreement without objection

18. EGLTNIABNI   18. I_____
                      Not able to be seen or touched

19. ODITLIAANV   19. V_____
                      Confirmation; support by facts

20. SSEIU   20. I_____
                      Matter or point of discussion

VOCABULARY REVIEW SCRAMBLE 2 *Farewell to Manzanar*
Change the order of the letters to find the original word.

1. SEBLIKO
2. AILLFI
3. IISNE
4. RUQTEESOG
5. GNUGOIG
6. CEAUSTOIRNP
7. OCSTOEINNG
8. ACNSTE
9. INEDSEDRC
10. USSLUPR
11. SBAI
12. SMSAP
13. TVIONOIL
14. IGLENVTAI
15. ENITRTNMEN
16. NMROEAOD
17. WNDLEDI
18. IILVD
19. HOSPOMUSTU
20. ISULOFHR

21. O_____
    Tapering, four-sided structure with a pyramid-shaped top
22. F_____
    Of a son or daughter
23. N_____
    Second generation; Japanese born in US before WWII
24. G_____
    Ridiculous; absurd
25. G_____
    Digging; tearing out
26. P_____
    Care taken beforehand
27. C_____
    An over-crowded condition
28. S_____
    Manner of standing
29. R_____
    Canceled
30. S_____
    Extra
31. B_____
    Preference based on prejudice
32. S_____
    Involuntary muscle contraction
33. V_____
    Decision or choice
34. V_____
    Someone who takes the law into his own hands
35. I_____
    Being forced to stay in a place
36. M_____
    Left in a helpless condition
37. D_____
    Make or become smaller or fewer
38. L_____
    Extremely angry
39. P_____
    Happening after one's death
40. F_____
    A showy display

ANSWER KEY JUGGLE LETTER REVIEW *Farewell to Manzanar*

	WORKSHEET 1	WORKSHEET 2
1	CUBICLES	OBELISK
2	OVERT	FILIAL
3	ALIENS	NISEI
4	EMIGRATION	GROTESQUE
5	HUNKER	GOUGING
6	CONFISCATORS	PRECAUTIONS
7	SABOTEUR	CONGESTION
8	OBSTINANCE	STANCE
9	INCONGRUOUS	RESCINDED
10	ASSIMILATE	SURPLUS
11	WARDING	BIAS
12	CAREENING	SPASM
13	TROUGH	VOLITION
14	NATURALIZATION	VIGILANTE
15	PATRIARCH	INTERNMENT
16	AUTHENTIC	MAROONED
17	ACQUIESCENCE	DWINDLE
18	INTANGIBLE	LIVID
19	VALIDATION	POSTHUMOUS
20	ISSUE	FLOURISH

VOCABULARY WORD LIST - Farewell to Manzanar

No.	Word	Clue/Definition
1.	ACQUIESCENCE	Agreement without objection
2.	AFFIRMED	Declared to be true
3.	AGITATING	Stirring up public awareness and feeling
4.	ALIENS	Non-citizens living in a country
5.	ASSIMILATE	Become like the others in custom, etc.
6.	ASUNDER	In pieces or separate parts
7.	AUTHENTIC	Real; genuine
8.	BARRACKS	Large, plain buildings used for temporary housing
9.	BENEVOLENT	Kindly; charitable
10.	BIAS	Preference based on prejudice
11.	CAPITULATE	Surrender on certain conditions
12.	CAREENING	Rushing headlong with a swaying motion
13.	CHAOS	Great confusion & disorder
14.	COLLABORATOR	One who cooperates treasonably, as with an enemy occupying one's country
15.	CONFISCATORS	Authorities who take and keep things
16.	CONGESTION	An over-crowded condition
17.	CREDO	Beliefs
18.	CRINGE	Crouch in fear
19.	CUBICLES	Very small rooms
20.	DISPERSING	Going away in different directions
21.	DREDGE	Bring up
22.	DWINDLE	Make or become smaller or fewer
23.	EDICTS	Rules proclaimed by one in authority
24.	EMIGRATION	Resettling in another country
25.	FILIAL	Of a son or daughter
26.	FLOURISH	A showy display
27.	GOUGING	Digging; tearing out
28.	GROTESQUE	Ridiculous; absurd
29.	GUILELESS	Honest; straightforward
30.	HUNKER	Squat; sit back on one's heels
31.	IDEALIST	One who wants things to be perfect
32.	IMPACT	Forceful effect
33.	IMPERIOUSLY	In an arrogant, domineering way
34.	INCONGRUOUS	Out of place
35.	INEVITABLE	Unavoidable
36.	INTANGIBLE	Not able to be seen or touched
37.	INTERNMENT	Being forced to stay in a place
38.	ISSEI	First generation; born in Japan
39.	ISSUE	Matter or point of discussion
40.	LIVID	Extremely angry
41.	MAROONED	Left in a helpless condition
42.	METAMORPHOSIS	Change of form or structure
43.	NATURALIZATION	Admitted to citizenship
44.	NISEI	Second generation; Japanese born in US before WWII
45.	OBELISK	Tapering, four-sided structure with a pyramid-shaped top
46.	OBLIVION	Condition of being entirely forgotten
47.	OBSTINANCE	Stubbornness
48.	OMINOUS	Unfavorable; threatening
49.	OVERT	Public; not hidden

VOCABULARY WORD LIST - Farewell to Manzanar continued

No. Word	Clue/Definition
50. PATRIARCH	Male head of family
51. PLACATOR	Peacemaker
52. POSTHUMOUS	Happening after one's death
53. POTENCY	Power; strength
54. PRECAUTIONS	Care taken beforehand
55. PREMONITIONS	Warnings of what is to come
56. PRIORITY	Coming in order of importance
57. RESCINDED	Canceled
58. RESERVOIR	Place where water is collected and stored
59. RESIGNED	Accepting what comes without complaint
60. SABOTEUR	Person who harms an enemy nation
61. SANSEI	Third generation; Japanese born in US after WWII
62. SEDATE	Calm, serious
63. SPASM	Involuntary muscle contraction
64. STANCE	Manner of standing
65. SUBDUED	Overcome by force; conquered
66. SURPLUS	Extra
67. SUSTENANCE	Nourishment or support
68. TINGE	A slight coloring
69. TROUGH	Narrow, open container holding water
70. TURBULENT	Violent
71. TURMOIL	State of agitation or disturbance
72. UNQUALIFIED	Complete; without lines or restrictions
73. VALIDATION	Confirmation; support by facts
74. VENTURE	Dare to go
75. VIGIL	Watching
76. VIGILANTE	Someone who takes the law into his own hands
77. VOLITION	Decision or choice
78. VULNERABILITY	Being open to attack or injury
79. WARDING	Keeping away

www.ingramcontent.com/pod-product-compliance
Lightning Source LLC
LaVergne TN
LVHW081533060526
838200LV00048B/2070

9781602491625